Puss In Boots

A Pantomime

John Crocker

A Samuel French Acting Edition

SAMUELFRENCH-LONDON.CO.UK
SAMUELFRENCH.COM

Copyright © 1967 by John Crocker (book) & Eric Gilder (lyric)
All Rights Reserved

PUSS IN BOOTS is fully protected under the copyright laws of the British Commonwealth, including Canada, the United States of America, and all other countries of the Copyright Union. All rights, including professional and amateur stage productions, recitation, lecturing, public reading, motion picture, radio broadcasting, television and the rights of translation into foreign languages are strictly reserved.

ISBN 978-0-573-16446-0

www.samuelfrench-london.co.uk

www.samuelfrench.com

FOR AMATEUR PRODUCTION ENQUIRIES

UNITED KINGDOM AND WORLD EXCLUDING NORTH AMERICA

plays@SamuelFrench-London.co.uk

020 7255 4302/01

Each title is subject to availability from Samuel French, depending upon country of performance.

CAUTION: Professional and amateur producers are hereby warned that *PUSS IN BOOTS* is subject to a licensing fee. Publication of this play does not imply availability for performance. Both amateurs and professionals considering a production are strongly advised to apply to the appropriate agent before starting rehearsals, advertising, or booking a theatre. A licensing fee must be paid whether the title is presented for charity or gain and whether or not admission is charged.

The professional rights in this play are controlled by Samuel French Ltd, 52 Fitzroy Street, London, W1T 5JR.

No one shall make any changes in this title for the purpose of production. No part of this book may be reproduced, stored in a retrieval system, or transmitted in any form, by any means, now known or yet to be invented, including mechanical, electronic, photocopying, recording, videotaping, or otherwise, without the prior written permission of the publisher. No one shall upload this title, or part of this title, to any social media websites.

The right of John Crocker to be identified as author of this work has been asserted by him in accordance with Section 77 of the Copyright, Designs and Patents Act 1988

PRODUCTION NOTE

Pantomime, as we know it today, is a form of entertainment all on its own, derived from a number of different sources - the commedia dell' arte (and all that that derived from), the ballet, the opera, the music hall and the realms of folk-lore and fairy tale. And elements of all of these are still to be found in it. This strange mixture has created a splendid topsy-turvy world where men are women, women are men, where the present is embraced within the past, where people are hit but not hurt, where authority is constantly flouted, where fun is poked at everything including pantomime itself at times and, above all, where magic abounds and dreams invariably come true. In other words, it is - or should be - fun. Fun to do and fun to watch and the sense of enjoyment which can be conveyed by a cast is very important to the enjoyment of the audience.

Pantomime can be very simply staged if resources are limited. Basically a tab surround at the back, tab legs at the sides and a set of traverse tabs for the frontcloth scenes, together with the simplest of small cut-out pieces to suggest the various locales - or even just placards with this information written on them - will suffice. Conversely, there is no limit to the extent to which more lavish facilities can be employed.

The directions I have given in the text adopt a middle course and are based on a permanent setting of a cyclorama skycloth at the back, a few feet in front of which is a rostrum about two feet high, running the width of the stage. About two thirds of the depth downstage is a false proscenium, immediately behind which are the lines for a set of traverse tabs. Below the false proscenium are arched entrances left and right, with possibly one foot reveals to the proscenium. A border will be necessary at some point between the false proscenium and the cyclorama to mask lighting battens and the top of the cyclorama. Lastly, there is a set of steps leading from the front of the stage into the auditorium, which I have referred to as the catwalk. I have imagined it to be set stage left, but it is unimportant whether it is left or right.

Into this permanent setting are placed various wings left and right; I have catered for one a side set on a level with the border, but a greater depth of stage may require two a side for masking purposes. Cut-out ground-rows set on the back of the rostrum complete the full sets. On smaller stages these cut-outs seen against the cyclorama give a better impression of depth than backcloths. The frontcloth fly lines come in behind the traverse tabs. Cloths can, of course, be tumbled or rolled if flying space is limited. It is a good tip always to bring in the traverse tabs when a cloth has to be lowered, then if any hitch occurs the lights can still come up and the actors get on with the scene. Similarly, I have indicated where the traverse tabs should be closed in frontcloth scenes so that there is plenty of time for the cloth to be flown before the end of the scene. The quick flow of one scene into the next is important if a smooth running production is to be achieved.

The settings and costumes should preferably be in clear bright colours to give a story book effect. It is probably best to try to have one overall period, but which period is immaterial. Also, of course, deliberate anachronisms should be introduced into some settings and some of the comics costumes. Animal skins can be hired from Theatre-Zoo, 21 Earlham Street, London WC2.

Pantomime requires many props and often they will have to be home made. Instructions are given in the prop plot for any of the more awkward seeming ones. Props should also be colourfully painted and in pantomime most props should be much larger than reality. It is wise for the property master to examine carefully the practical use to which a prop is to be put - it is very painful to be hit with a Giant's club of solid wood, one of material filled with foam plastic is far gentler!

I have not attempted to give a lighting plot as this entirely depends on the equipment available, but, generally speaking, most pantomime lighting needs to be full up, warm and bright. Pinks and ambers are probably best for this. Follow spots are a great help for this kind of show, but not essential. If they are available, though, it is often effective in romantic numbers to fade out the stage lighting and hold the principals in the follow spots, quickly fading up on the last few bars as this frequently helps to increase the applause! They can also be used for the Fairy and Demon to give them greater freedom of movement than with fixed front of house or spot-bar spots. Flash boxes, with the necessary colour and flash powders, can be obtained from the usual stage electrical suppliers.

The music has been specially composed so that it is easy for the less musically accomplished to master, but it is also scored in parts for the more ambitious. If an orchestra is available well and good, but a single piano will suffice. It is an advantage, however, if there can be a drummer as well. Not only because a rhythm accompaniment enhances the numbers, but also because for some reason never yet fully fathomed slapstick hits and falls are always twice as funny if they coincide with a well timed bonk on a drum, wood-block or whatever is found to make the noise best suited to the action. A drummer can also cope with the various "whizzes" and "tings" noted in the directions, though if necessary they can be done off stage. A special type of whistle can be got for the "whizz" and the "ting" requires a triangle.

Pantomime demands a particular style of playing and production. The acting must be larger than life, but still sincere, with a good deal of sparkle and attack. Much of it must be projected directly at the audience, since one of pantomime's great advantages is that it deliberately breaks down the "fourth wall". The actors can literally and metaphorically shake hands with their audience who become almost another member of the cast; indeed, their active participation from time to time is essential. A word of warning on this, though - the actors must always remain in control; for instance, if a Demon or villain encourages hissing he must make sure it is never to such an extent that he can no longer be heard. The producer should see that the story line is clearly brought out and treated with respect. There is always room for local gags and topical quips in pantomime, but they should not be overdone. Most important of all, the comedy, as any comedy, must never appear to be conscious of its own funniness.

Characterization should be very clear and definite. I prefer the traditional use of a man to play the Dame and a girl to play the Principal Boy. In the case of the Dame, anyway, there is a sound argument for this - audiences will laugh more readily at a man impersonating a woman involved in the mock cruelties of slapstick than at a real woman. For this reason an actor playing a Dame should never quite let us forget he is a man, while giving a sincere character performance of a woman; further, he can be as feminine as he likes, but never effeminate. Queen Marmaduchess should be played with great relish and with great dignity at the same time. Her graciousness springs from her tolerance and good nature and even her dominance over her husband is based more on affection than any desire to dominate.

A Principal Boy also requires a character performance, but, of course, with the implications reversed! An occasional slap of the thigh is not sufficient. Philip should be thought of as a very charming, unsophisticated young man. He asks for little, but gains a lot. His innate honesty is much disturbed by what he imagines to be his false pose as a Marquis.

Principal Girls can be a bore, but only if they are presented as mere pretty symbols of feminine sweetness. Princess Esmerelda should appear roguish and high spirited. She is naturally outspoken, a trait which is sharpened when she falls under the Demon's spell to make her proud. But her sense of humour should save her from losing the audience's sympathy when this occurs.

Puss is played by two people - one as the Mime Puss, in a complete cat skin and mask, the other as the talking Puss in a skin-tight representational costume with a half mask or even no mask at all and may well be best played by a girl. This is perhaps because Puss is such a complete realist; he has no romantic notions, no false modesty, knows exactly what he wants and always gets it. His attitude to Philip is patronising, but only in the way that cats are always patronising to their masters. The other "animal", Neddy the donkey, is less serious minded. His waywardness comes from his love of fun, coupled with that streak of obstinacy normal in donkeys.

Jimothy is willing to turn his hand to anything - he has to be. But his wry sense of humour and a certain detachment prevent him from feeling any resentment that his good nature may be being exploited. It is a part which an actor can very much invest with his own charm and personality. His girl friend, Mistress Mary Quite Contrary, should be very pretty to carry off her solemnity. She must have great conviction in the rightness of her inside-out approach to life and pursue it with determination.

King Marmaduke has a mind which jumps to the next thought before the first one is uttered. To ensure that these unexpressed thoughts are conveyed to the audience in some measure he must have them clearly implanted in his own mind and must not appear merely vague. On the other hand his Court Chamberlain, Lord Snoozle, is decidedly vague; he lives in a world of his own, where the barriers between sleeping and waking hardly exist.

Phiddle is not really up to his picture of himself as a particularly clever cunning fellow. He continually trips up over his own - and Phaddle's - shortcomings. Conversely, Phaddle has no false ideas about himself. Indeed, ideas altogether are somewhat beyond him - he has an essentially literal mind.

Rowley is a hypochondriac. His deep interest in his own well being has given him a rather humourless, sad outlook on life. His part can be doubled with the Ogre if desired. Greedyguts is very blustering and brusque, like a testy colonel. His pride in his powers as a magician is not well founded, the results are always hit or miss. This makes him sensitive to criticism and an easy prey to flattery - hence his downfall.

The immortals are not at all devoid of very mortal emotions; they enjoy a childish glee in scoring off each other and indulge in equally childish rudeness when scored off. Theirs is the eternal struggle between opposites; in this case not only good and evil but age and youth as well. But, as there so often is, beneath the enmity there is also a kind of affection.

I have made provision for a Chorus of six, but naturally the number used will depend on how many are available.

John Crocker.

CHARACTERS

ANTHONY ROWLEY	
PRINCESS ESMERELDA	
JIMOTHY	The King's Page
MISTRESS MARY QUITE CONTRARY	
PHIDDLE	
PHADDLE	The Miller's Sons
PHILIP	
NEDDY	A Donkey
MIME PUSS	
PUSS	Philip's Cat
KING MARMADUKE	
QUEEN MARMADUCHESS	
SPRITE YOUNGOOD	
DEMON OLDBAD	
LORD SNOOZLE	The Court Chamberlain
GREEDYGUTS	The Wicked Ogre

CHORUS as Villagers, Courtiers, Birds, Insects, Bats, Vassals, etc.

SYNOPSIS OF SCENES

PART ONE

Scene One	Outside the Old Mill in Marmaladia.
Scene Two	A Woodland Glade.
Scene Three	The Audience Chamber at the Palace
Scene Four	A Street outside the Palace.
Scene Five	The Orange Grove beside the Lake.

PART TWO

Scene Six	The Ballroom at the Palace.
Scene Seven	Outside the Palace.
Scene Eight	The Royal Barracks.
Scene Nine	On the way to Grislykeep.
Scene Ten	Grislykeep, the Ogre's Castle.
Scene Eleven	Rewards and Fairies.
Scene Twelve	The Wedding Reception of the Marquess and Marchioness of Carabas.

Running time: Approximately two hours and thirty-five minutes.

(MUSIC 1. OVERTURE.)

PART ONE

Scene One - OUTSIDE THE OLD MILL IN MARMALADIA

(Fullset. Village wings L. and R. Cut-out ground-row at back of rostrum showing suitable background to Mill piece set to L.C. on rostrum. Mill fitted with practical door opening up and downstage, steps down in front of door. Large filled flour sack set C. Large prop flower-pot in front of pros. arch R. CHORUS, as village lads and lasses, and ANTHONY ROWLEY discovered.)

MUSIC 2. "MARMALADIA"

CHORUS & ROWLEY:
We're citizens of Marmaladia
Here assembled to say "Good-day" to ya.
We're a corner of Arcadia,
    With a comic King.
It's an old Marmaladian custom,
He makes laws and the populace bust 'em!
Hence today in Marmaladia,
    We don't do a thing
    But simply stand around and sing.

ROWLEY: Heigh.

1st CHORUS: What did you say, Roly-Poly?

ROWLEY: Heigh. After all, my name is Anthony Rowley so I'm really supposed to say "heigho", but I can't say heigho nowadays.

(CHORUS laugh.)

I can only get as far as heigh.

2nd CHORUS: Why?

ROWLEY: I've got hay fever. Heigh - heigh - heigh - TISHOO! You see. It's all this working in the orange groves. And we ought to be there now, really, to try and gather everything in before that old Ogre Greedy-guts steals it.

3rd CHORUS: Well, he always does steal the crop however hard we try, so why worry?

4th CHORUS: I think we'd better. Here comes the Princess, she might tell the King.

ROWLEY & CHORUS: The Princess! Quick! Over here! No, over here! Etc.

(Some hide behind Mill, others behind wing R.)

5th CHORUS: Come on, Roly-Poly, behind this flour sack!

ROWLEY: Oh no, not there! My hay-fever, it'll make me sneeze.

6th CHORUS: Don't argue, Roly-Poly!

(5th and 6th CHORUS push ROWLEY, still protesting, behind sack and

(hide with him. MUSIC 3. Enter PRINCESS ESMERELDA L.)

PRINCESS: That's curious. I thought there was somebody here. (sees the others hiding) No, of course, they'll all be hard at work gathering oranges.

(ROWLEY rises, obviously about to sneeze. 5th and 6th CHORUS rise and put their fingers under his nose.)

Oh, I do believe I'm going to sneeze.

(The three sink out of sight.)

Oh no, I'm not.

(Loud sneeze from ROWLEY which knocks over sack.)

Oh, but I did. Well, I never, people.

(ROWLEY and all CHORUS emerge sheepishly. ROWLEY sneezes.)

Oh dear, somebody else sneezing. Poor thing, he must have caught it from me.

ROWLEY: No, I didn't, I caught it from the heigh - heigh - heigh - TISHOO! - the flour sacks.

PRINCESS: Then whyever were you hiding there?

1st CHORUS: Because we should be working and we - er -

ROWLEY: We're not - Atishoo!

PRINCESS: (shaking head) Tut, tut. I can't think what father will say, especially since -

ROWLEY: Oh dear, since what, your Highness?

PRINCESS: Since he's declared today a public holiday!

ROWLEY & CHORUS: What?

PRINCESS: Yes, to celebrate my coming of age.

CHORUS: Oh, hurrah! Congratulations! Etc.

ROWLEY: Yes, congra - gra - gra - Achoo!

PRINCESS: Bless you. I'm sure Jimothy would have told you sometime, but poor Jimothy has to do nearly everything now, though he's only supposed to be father's page. Father did say something about trying to get me a Maid of Honour, but it probably won't come to anything. It's all the fault of that beastly Greedyguts. It's most inconvenient having an Ogre who likes oranges living here when all we do is make marmalade. I shall really have to change all that when I become Queen. There's quite a few other things I'd like to change too, but lots I don't want to change at all.

MUSIC 4. "CHANGES"

If I could do anything under the sun,
I might change the way that the world was run;

(continued)

        But I wouldn't change the way the flowers come in Spring,
           Nor the Autumn leaves start to fall,
        And I wouldn't change the way that little children sing -
           I would not change much at all.

        If I were possessed of a magical power,
        I might squeeze a year into half an hour;
        But I wouldn't change the music of a Summer night,
           Nor the sound of a ragman's call,
        And I wouldn't even change the way that kittens bite -
           I would not change much at all.

        If you should want to fly with wings
           I might try to arrange it;
        But don't give me a five-pound note,
           'Cos I simply <u>couldn't</u> change it!

        I might change the way that some old people fuss,
        I might change the time of the local bus;
        But I wouldn't change the lovely presents I have had,
           Nor the way that the grass grows tall;
        When you come to think that life is really not so bad,
           I would not change much at all.

(exits R.)

JIMOTHY: (off L.) Oyez! Oyez! Oyez!

CHORUS: It's Jimothy! Hullo, Jimothy!

(<u>MUSIC 5</u>. Enter JIMOTHY U.L., carrying a large prop silver bell and three scrolls. He moves to C.)

JIMOTHY: Ssh! I'm not Jimothy at the moment. I mean, I am, but I'm also the town crier.

(Raises bell to ring it. CHORUS and ROWLEY put their hands over their ears. He rings bell, it only sounds a tiny tinkle - (little bell fitted inside). They uncover their ears, surprised.

Oyez! (rings bell more determinedly) CHORUS laugh.

OYEZ! (rings bell even harder then throws it down in disgust. It lands on his foot. Clasps foot in pain) Oh, help!

(CHORUS laugh.)

I'll continue without the musical accompaniment. (reading from one scroll) Er-hm. Citizens of Marmaladia -

ROWLEY: I say.

JIMOTHY: Yes?

ROWLEY: If it's about the Princess coming of age, we know.

I - 1 - 4

JIMOTHY: Oh. Well, I'll get on with the next announcement then. (throws scroll off and prepares to read another) Er-hm. Citizens -

ROWLEY: I say.

JIMOTHY: Now what?

ROWLEY: If it's about today being a holiday, we know that too.

JIMOTHY: Oh. I'll do the last announcement then. (throws scroll off and prepares to read from last one) Er-hm -

ROWLEY: I say.

(JIMOTHY throws scrolls off.)

BOTH: We/You know about the Princess wanting a Maid of Honour.

JIMOTHY: I'm beginning to feel redundant. Still, since you all know about it, perhaps one of you would like to volunteer.

CHORUS: Oh yes, please. Me, please. No, me. Me, Jimothy. Etc.

2nd CHORUS: Is it worth a lot of money, Jimothy?

JIMOTHY: No, that's what the honour bit means. You do it for nothing.

CHORUS: Oh dear.

3rd CHORUS: But there wouldn't be much to do, would there?

JIMOTHY: We-ll, not really. Apart from waiting on the Princess, there'd only be the royal shopping, the royal cooking, washing-up, laundering, ironing, mending, scrubbing, sweeping, dusting, polishing, boot-cleaning, bed-making -

(During this speech CHORUS back towards sides of stage.)

CHORUS: Help! (They run off L. and R.)

JIMOTHY: I was afraid that would happen.

ROWLEY: I say, could I be a Maid of Honour?

JIMOTHY: I don't think you're quite suitable, Rowley. You have to be a girl.

ROWLEY: Oh. I don't think I could manage that. Pity, I'm sure it would have been much better for my hay - hay - hay - tishoo! (exits R. Puts head on again) Fever. (goes)

JIMOTHY: Well, now who am I going to try?

(MUSIC 6. MISTRESS MARY QUITE CONTRARY enters L., backwards and collides with JIMOTHY.)

Oops, sorry.

MARY: Not at all, but next time look where I'm going. (moves on, still walking backwards)

JIMOTHY: Yes, I will. Eh? Here, you're walking the wrong way round.

MARY: (circling round to come back again) Not at all. As far as I'm concerned, this is the right way round. (crashes into his L. side again and stops with back to him) Dear, dear, you're still not looking where I'm going.

JIMOTHY: Now wait a minute, who do you think you are?

MARY: I am Mistress Mary Quite Contrary. I'm a horticultural expert.

JIMOTHY: I see. Well, I'm Jimothy, the King's page. What is a horti - er - horti-what-you-said?

MARY: In common parlance, a horticultural expert is a gardener.

JIMOTHY: Oh. And how does your garden grow?

MARY: It doesn't. My last employer objected to what I wished to plant. Not that it was anything very extraordinary. Just a row of pretty maids, with some cockle shells and silver bells. I was planting them to build up the tourist trade, of course.

JIMOTHY: I - er - don't quite follow.

MARY: I should have thought it was obvious. If you want tourists you must attract them, and what could be more attractive than a row of pretty maids? And to feed the tourists what could be better than good nourishing cockles?

JIMOTHY: And the silver bells?

MARY: For the tourists' landladies to ring at mealtime, of course.

JIMOTHY: Oh, yes, silly of me. But how do you grow things like silver bells?

MARY: Simple. Just plant the clapper.

JIMOTHY: Oh no, you're having me on. I've got a silver bell here but - well, I'll try it. (pulls clapper out of bell and sees flower pot by R. pros arch) Ah, that's handy. (puts clapper into flower pot) I bet it doesn't work, though.

(A plant with little silver bells grows from pot. **EFFECTS 1**. Bells jingle.

Ooh, it does. I must have silver fingers. The only thing is, how am I going to look after it?

MARY: It looks after itself. It rings an alarm if you touch it.

JIMOTHY: Really? I'll try that.

(Puts out hand to plant. **EFFECTS 2**. Bells jingle.)

Oh yes, rather a pretty little noise, but it is only a little noise, I mightn't hear it. I know, I'll ask all these people here to help. (to AUDIENCE) I say, if anybody tries to steal my bell plant and it starts ringing, will you help it by shouting "Silver Bells"? You will? Good. Let's have a little practice then. I'll hide and Mistress Mary will pretend to steal it.

(Runs off D.R. MARY creeps backwards to plant and touches it,

I - 1 - 6

(encouraging AUDIENCE to shout. EFFECTS 3. Bells jingle. JIMOTHY runs on.)

JIMOTHY: (continued) I heard a faint whisper. I expect you were a bit confused because she walks backwards, but don't let that worry you. Just imagine she's someone else walking forwards. We'll try again.

(Runs off. Same process as before. EFFECTS 4.)

Better, better, much better, but I'm sure you can do even better still. Let's try just once more for luck.

(Runs off. Same process as before. EFFECTS 5.)

Oh, very good. Now I know it'll be quite safe.

MARY: Well, I must go and let a job look for me.

JIMOTHY: Wait a bit, there's a job going at Court.

MARY: Very well, I'll take it.

JIMOTHY: The only thing is it's as a Maid of Honour - you wouldn't get any money.

MARY: That's all right, I'll grow my own mint.

JIMOTHY: Very wise of you.

MARY: Oh no, I'm not wise. I'm contrariwise.

MUSIC 7. "THE WISE ONES"

    People say that I'll never marry;
    I never tarry with lighter ones.
    Though there's wickedness in my eyes,
        I'm not so very wise.

JIMOTHY:
    People say that I'm sort of soppy;
    I never copy the brighter ones.
    Friends all tell me that for my size
        I'm not so very wise.

BOTH:
    Looks, we feel, are most deceiving.
    Seeing things is not believing.

MARY: I love him.

JIMOTHY: And she loves me,

BOTH:
    And that is as clever as clever can be!
    There's a matter we ought to mention;
        Without dissention our future lies.
    Matrimony is our intention -
        And that is very wise.

    Do not take us as you see us -
        Though we both look pretty dim.
    We are very pleased to be us.

JIMOTHY: I love her.

I-1-7

MARY:	And she loves him.
JIMOTHY:	People say, etc.)
MARY:	Do not take us, etc.) (together)
BOTH:	Do not judge us from our faces; Circumstances alter cases.
MARY:	I've got him.
JIMOTHY:	And she's got me.
BOTH:	And we are as happy as happy could be. There's just one item in conclusion To save confusion that might arise: We'll grow old in complete collusion - And that is very wise.

(Both exit backwards L. MUSIC 8. Enter PHADDLE R., pulling hard on a rope that goes over his shoulder and offstage.)

PHADDLE: Come on, Neddy, good donkey, nice donkey, come on.

(Moves up steps to Mill door and drags on PHIDDLE who has the other end of the rope round his neck and is trying hard to prevent himself being strangled. PHADDLE knocks on Mill door.)

Hey, Phiddle, I've got Neddy for you. Phiddle!

PHIDDLE: Yes, Phaddle?

PHADDLE: (turning in surprise) Hullo, Phiddle. What are you doing there?

PHIDDLE: Strangling. Let go of the rope.

PHADDLE: Oh no, Neddy might run away if I did that.

PHIDDLE: I am not Neddy, you nit. I am your brother, Phiddle.

PHADDLE: I know you're my brother. I mean, you always have been.

PHIDDLE: Yes, but I shan't be much longer, if you don't let go of that rope.

PHADDLE: Mind you, I've got another brother too, Philip. But he's not here now. He went away for a year and a day after father died. And when he comes back we shall be able to find out what was in father's will.

PHIDDLE: Yes, yes, yes. I remember it all quite clearly, let go -

PHADDLE: I've got other things besides brothers too. I've got guppies. They're fish, little black fish. (moving towards PHIDDLE) I say, I've just noticed something.

PHIDDLE: At last.

PHADDLE: (ignoring PHIDDLE and crossing him) Yes, there are some little silver bells growing on a plant. I think I'll take one.

(Puts out hand to do so. EFFECTS 6. Bells jingle. AUDIENCE shout. PHADDLE runs back up steps in alarm, pulling rope tight again.

(JIMOTHY runs on D.R.)

JIMOTHY: Ah, saved by the bell, thank you. Phiddle, that was very naughty of you trying to pinch one of my silver bells.

PHIDDLE: But I - I -

JIMOTHY: Now, now, no stories. (exits R.)

PHIDDLE: See what you've done? Got me into trouble again. And LET GO OF THAT ROPE! You're ruining my neck.

PHADDLE: Well, you shouldn't have put your neck in the rope.

PHIDDLE: I didn't. You told me you could lasso Neddy with your eyes shut. Well, you can't. Now get me out of it.

(PHADDLE moves down and helps PHIDDLE out of rope and throws it off.)

About time too. Now we need Neddy.

PHADDLE: Why?

PHIDDLE: Because I'm taking up a life of crime. I want lots of money. We haven't made much with the mill since father died, so I'm going to be a highwayman and I want Neddy to ride.

PHADDLE: Ooh, he won't like that. Couldn't you be something else?

PHIDDLE: No, I've only got to save another two cornflake packet tops and I can get a highwayman's mask and pistol.

PHADDLE: What, a real pistol, one that goes bang?

PHIDDLE: No, actually it goes snap, crackle, pop. But never mind that now. Go and get the saddle.

PHADDLE: All right. (exits into Mill)

PHIDDLE: (opening door upstage and calling) Bring the bridle too. (shuts door)

(PHADDLE opens door D.S. and knocks PHIDDLE down steps.)

PHADDLE: What did you say? That's funny, I thought he was still here. (goes, shutting door)

PHIDDLE: (rising and running up steps) Hey, come back.

(PHADDLE opens door and knocks PHIDDLE down again.)

PHADDLE: What for? Oh. He's gone again.

PHIDDLE: (crawling forward on all fours) I have not. (rises and moves up steps) I'm trying to tell you to bring the bridle as well, but you keep knocking me down with the door.

PHADDLE: Do I? Well next time I'll open it this way (pushes door U.S.), instead of that way.

(Pushes door D.S., knocking PHADDLE down steps.)

Oops, sorry. (goes, shutting door)

I-1-9

PHIDDLE: Sometimes I think - what would I do without him? It's a lovely thought, too. What was he saying about this plant? Ooh, he's right. It has got silver bells on it. I'll help myself to a few.

(Puts hand out. EFFECTS 7. Bells jingle. AUDIENCE shout. PHIDDLE runs up steps and JIMOTHY opens Mill door D.S. knocking him down.)

JIMOTHY: Ah, caught you again! (to AUDIENCE) Thank you. (goes, shutting door)

PHIDDLE: How did he get there?

(PHADDLE enters from Mill with saddle and bridle.)

PHADDLE: Here you are.

PHIDDLE: Good. (takes bridle)

NEDDY: (off L.) EE-AW!

PHIDDLE: Ah, Neddy.

(MUSIC 9. NEDDY trots on L. and comes to C.)

NEDDY: Ee-aw! (crosses R. foreleg over L. and bows to them. Crosses L. over R. and bows to AUDIENCE)

PHIDDLE: What a bit of luck you've arrived, Neddy. We're going to saddle you.

(NEDDY shakes head firmly.)

Yes, we are.

(NEDDY shakes head and stamps foreleg.)

PHADDLE: I said he wouldn't like it.

PHIDDLE: (sotto voce) We'll take him by surprise then.

PHADDLE: How?

PHIDDLE: Well, first, I'll... (mumbles incomprehensibly in PHADDLE's ear)

(NEDDY cocks an ear up trying to hear.)

And you'll... (mumbles again)

PHADDLE: But what about him?

PHIDDLE: Oh, he'll -

(As he leans forward to whisper again NEDDY shoots out a front and rear-leg to kick PHIDDLE and PHADDLE, who fall with a cry and NEDDY runs off below wing L.

PHIDDLE: Quick! After him! Grab his tail!

(They dive after him and land offstage. EFFECTS 8. Banging and clattering off L.)

PHADDLE: (off L.) Got him! Ouch! Almost got the saddle on!

(NEDDY reappears above wing L.)

PHADDLE: (continued) There, it's on! (runs on below wing) Phiddle, he's ready, he's (sees NEDDY) Oh.

(PHIDDLE enters L., saddled and bridled. NEDDY tosses his head and gambols off R.)

PHIDDLE: I've gone right off being a highwayman. (removes saddle and bridle and throws them off L.)

PHILIP: (off R.) Hey, whoa there, Neddy!

PHIDDLE: Philip!

(MUSIC 10. PHILIP enters R., with arm affectionately round NEDDY, who is obviously delighted to see him.)

Well, this is a surprise. Welcome home.

(NEDDY nods and nuzzles PHILIP.)

PHILIP: Thank you, Phiddle, and you, Neddy. There's only Puss missing. You go and tell him to come and say hello.

(NEDDY nods and skips off L.)

PHIDDLE: We thought you were going to be away for a year and a day.

PHILIP: So I have been.

PHIDDLE: Have you? In that case, we'd better get on with reading the will, and it just so happens I've got it with me. (whips out a very dog-eared looking document) Ah, many's the time I've been tempted to read this while you've been away, but my principles wouldn't let me.

PHADDLE: I thought it was because you can't read.

PHIDDLE: Sharrup! Can't you see Philip wants to see the state of his estate? (thrusts will into PHILIP's hands) What have I been left?

PHILIP: Er - the Mill.

PHIDDLE: Yes - and?

PHILIP: The donkey. Oh no, that's Phaddle's share.

PHIDDLE: It would be. But the money? Don't I - I mean, don't any of us get any money? What's he left you?

PHILIP: Well, I don't quite understand it. It's a sort of riddle. Listen.

> "And so then to my last bequest.
> I leave the brass and oaken chest (turns page)
> To Philip. Yet no gift this is,
> For I but give him what is his.
> A heritage that's barren now,
> But time will make it rich enow
> Provided he of Puss takes care,
> Since Puss for him did service rare."

What do you make of that?

PHIDDLE: Nothing, except you get the chest and the cat. But isn't there anything about money?

PHILIP: No, of course, there may be some in the chest.

PHIDDLE: That's it! I bet it's stuffed with money, hundreds of pounds worth! Thousands! Are you sure he left it to you and not me?

PHILIP: It says Philip here, but if there is any we'll share it. (returns will)

PHIDDLE: Just what I was going to suggest. Phaddle and I will go and look for you right away. Come on, Phaddle. (rushes to Mill, propelling PHADDLE before him.) Nice to have you back. Bye-bye.

(Exeunt into Mill shutting door. PHADDLE reappears, opening door D.S. and comes down steps.)

PHADDLE: Bye-bye from me too.

(PHIDDLE rushes out and pushes him into Mill.)

PHIDDLE: Don't waste time. (shuts door leaving himself outside) Ooh, left meself behind now.

(Opens door D.S. onto himself revealing PHADDLE patiently waiting.)

Ouch! I told you not to do that. (dashes into Mill and shuts door)

PHILIP: Well, I can see they haven't changed much.

PUSS: (off L.) Miaow!

PHILIP: Puss! My dear Puss!

(MUSIC 11. MIME PUSS enters L., riding on NEDDY. He puts up a languid paw for NEDDY to stop in C.)

(laughing) Well, I don't think father need have bothered to tell me to take care of you - you can take care of yourself.

(MIME PUSS agrees, then slides gracefully off NEDDY, indicates his thanks for the ride with a slight inclination of the head and moves to PHILIP holding out a paw to shake.)

Oh, very formal, aren't we? (shakes the paw) How do you do? Have you been a good boy while I've been away?

(MIME PUSS nods thoughtfully, then slyly shakes head)

PHILIP: Yes and no, eh? Perhaps it's just as well I'm back.

(MIME PUSS rubs head affectionately against PHILIP's legs.)

Ah, thank you, Puss.

NEDDY: Ee-aw!

PHILIP: And you Neddy. (pats him) And I'm certainly pleased to be home again.

MUSIC 12. "HOME"

I've just ended a wander.

(continued)
>
> I'm a back-of-beyonder.
>   All the world I've tried to comb,
> Now I've seen all the places under the worldly sky,
>   I'll be staying at home.
> Home's the nicest of places;
> Home's the friendliest faces;
>   Home's the ultimate place to go.
> Now I solemnly swear that I'll never say "Goodbye",
>   For home's the place where you say "Hullo".
>
> Home's the place where my bed is;
> Home's the home of the Neddies,
>   Where they greet me and say "Ee-aw".
> Home's the place where I find my silly old Puss again -
>   Come, Puss, give me your paw.
> All my life I have known you;
> I could never disown you -
>   Why I left I shall never know!
> Now you've opened the door I'm coming out of the
>   rain -
>   For home's the place where you say "Hullo".

(During number CHORUS enter to greet PHILIP. PHILIP exits into Mill with PUSS. Exit NEDDY R. ROWLEY runs on L.)

ROWLEY: Help! Help! The King and Queen are out driving again! Run for your lives!

(MUSIC 13. EFFECTS 9. Hooting and general clatter off L. CHORUS shriek and run off R., with ROWLEY. KING MARMADUKE comes panting in L. pushing a soap-box go-cart, which is being steered by QUEEN MARMADUCHESS, who is also tooting the hooter attached to it and graciously waving in the royal manner.)

QUEEN: Let her rip, Marmaduke!
KING: Yes, my love.

(They whizz off U.R. EFFECTS 10. LOUD GLASS CRASH R. They re-enter backwards.)

QUEEN: Bother that lampost.

(They exit L. EFFECTS 11. LOUD GLASS CRASH L. They re-enter.)

And that one. (steers round to face L.) Stop, far enough.

KING: What? Not fast enough?

(QUEEN has put her feet out and stopped as he speaks and now rises bending forward as he bends lower to push harder and jabs her in the rear with the points of his crown.)

QUEEN: (leaping aside, U.S.) OW! Marmaduke!

(As she leaps aside he jerks forward and falls flat, sending the go-cart off L. as he does so.)

KING: (rising) That's funny, we suddenly stopped all of - er - rather sharp.

QUEEN: (rubbing behind) Very sharp. I was nearly hit by one of those lamposts too. You must do something about having them moved, Marmaduke.

KING: Yes, of course, I - er -

(Lampost falls on stage R., followed by another one L.)

Don't think I need bother.

QUEEN: We'd better tidy them up. The Borough Council is a little lax in these matters.

(Music whizzes as lamposts are whisked off L. and R.)

Ah, they're getting more efficient.

(KING re-enters L.)

Oh, Marmaduke, look at that plant. I must have one of those dear little silver bells.

(Bends forward to take one. EFFECTS 12. Bells jingle. AUDIENCE shout. JIMOTHY and MARY run on backwards L.)

JIMOTHY: Coming, coming, thank you, thank -

(They bump into KING and send him plunging forward so that he rams QUEEN's behind with crown.)

QUEEN: (clutching behind) Marmaduke, really!

KING: Sorry, my dear, but I was just standing minding my own - er - all of a sudden shoved in my - er - landed on your - well, you get the point.

QUEEN: Very forcibly. I shan't be able to sit on my dignity for weeks. Ah, Jimothy, where have you suddenly sprung from, dear lad?

JIMOTHY: Well, your Majesty, those people shout for me if anybody tries to take my bell plant.

KING: What people? Not a soul in - er - so there is.

QUEEN: Oh, yes. And all sitting in the dark as good as gold. How quaint. Does this young lady come from down there?

MARY: No, but you're delighted to meet me. (shaking their hands) I'm your new Gardener of Honour, Mistress Mary Quite Contrary. How don't you don't?

QUEEN: Oh, very thank, well you. (reacts) I thought it was a Maid of Honour we wanted. Still, what are her qualifications?

JIMOTHY: Well, she's very good at walking backwards.

QUEEN: Most useful at court. What else?

JIMOTHY: She'll do the job for nothing.

QUEEN: Exactly the type of girl we need. She may start at once.

I - 1 - 14

MARY: Good. Now about the tourist trade -

JIMOTHY: Ssh! Not now. (pulling MARY with him and bowing out backwards) Excuse us, your Majesties.

(KING and QUEEN nod graciously as they run off backwards L.)

QUEEN: Charming girl. (peers at AUDIENCE) Marmaduke, why do you think all those people are sitting in the dark? Ah, I've got it, they must come from a country where it's still nighttime. I wonder if they speak any Marmaladian. (to AUDIENCE, very slowly and articulately, with illustrative hand gestures) Do you speak Marmaladian? I am speaking Marmaladian now. I will give you the customary Marmaladian greeting. Hul-lo. Can you say "Hul-lo"?

(AUDIENCE reaction)

Oh, splendid! Weren't they splendid, Marmaduke?

KING: Yes, extremely - er - spoke very - er - fluent.

QUEEN: Obviously a very musical people too - they've brought their own band. (to CONDUCTOR) Hul-lo.

CONDUCTOR: Hul-lo.

QUEEN: Well done! What - is - your - name?

CONDUCTOR: (Gives name.)

QUEEN: How extraordinary, quite Marmaladian. I wonder, (repeats name), would you like to play some music for us, and then we could say some words at the same time and it would be what we call a song in our language.

CONDUCTOR: Certainly, delighted to oblige.

QUEEN: (to KING) What a nice man.

(Intro starts. MUSIC 14.)

Oh, how touching, he's playing our National Anthem.

"ANTHEM"

BOTH: Bow your heads and bend the knee
To royalty dynastic.
Very modern rulers we
Our crowns are made of plastic.

QUEEN: Such impressive Queens as I
The royal line enhance.
He is King, but I'm the one
Who wears the royal pants.

BOTH: Grovel, all you commoners,
And kneel, you people trusty.
But first lay down a handkerchief
Because the floor is dusty.

I - 1 - 15

KING:	I've been king for - let me see - Well just - oh no, that's wrong. Of course upon the throne I've - yes, For nearly twice that long.
BOTH:	Blow the trumpets, roll the drums, Let royal cannon roar. Bow your heads and bend the knee.
KING:	We said that line before.
BOTH:	Lift your hearts and blow your noses, Let the people sing. Send a cheque in homage To your royal Queen and King

(Encore)

KING: My court is partly middle-class
But more especially upper.

QUEEN: I'm home alternate Saturdays -
Pop in and have a cuppa.

(And repeat final stanza)

(They exit L. MIME PUSS enters from Mill, sits on steps and starts to wash.)

PRINCESS: (Off R.) Mother! Father!

(As she runs on R., EFFECTS 13. Glass crash off L.)

Oh, bother, I've missed them. Hullo, Puss.

(PUSS ignores her.)

Well, you're not very friendly, are you?

(MIME PUSS spares her the briefest of glances and continues washing, then stops, looks at her again, puts a paw on top of his head to indicate "thinks", looks at Mill, then walks slowly round her eyeing her closely from all points of view.)

I hope I meet with your approval.

MIME PUSS: (considers for a beat, then nods and goes to Mill door) Miaow!

PRINCESS: And it seems a pity just after we've met, but I've got to go now.

MIME PUSS: (shakes head vehemently, indicates with a paw that she must stay where she is. Through Mill door.) MIAOW!

PHILIP: (off) Coming. (appearing in Mill doorway) What is it Puss?

(MIME PUSS points imperiously at PRINCESS, gives PHILIP a push towards her and exits L.)

Oh, I'm so sorry. Did you want some flour or something?

PRINCESS: No, but your cat seemed to think we should meet.

PHILIP: Oh dear, I'm afraid he's rather bossy sometimes. Still, it's not a bad idea, is it? How do you do? My name's Philip. I'm a miller.

PRINCESS: How do you do? Mine's Esmerelda. I'm a Princess.

PHILIP: Oh. I beg your pardon, your Highness. Maybe it wasn't such a good idea.

PRINCESS: I think it was an excellent one.

PHILIP: But I mean, we're not quite sort of equal, are we?

PRINCESS: Well, I'm not proud even if you are. And your cat approved of me.

PHILIP: Ah, yes, but a cat may look at a king.

PRINCESS: Then why shouldn't a miller look at a Princess?

MUSIC 15. "WHOEVER YOU ARE"

> Whoever you are it's nice to see you.
> Whoever you are I like the view.
> I'm sure that it must
> Be nice to be you
> But it's nice being me
> Looking at you.
>
> Perhaps you may be my next door neighbour,
> Perhaps you have tumbled from a star.
> But one thing's certain from the moment that we met,
> I've fallen in love, whoever you are.

(They exit L. MUSIC 16 starting quietly, growing in volume. Lights fade to white spot R. SPRITE YOUNGOOD enters R., rather breathless. She is very young, has no wings and carries a very short wand.

SPRITE: Oh bother! Blow! I fear I'm late,
Young Philip's heart has met it's fate.
Youngood's my name and, mortals, please
Grant pardon that I gasp and wheeze.
But I 'neath beating midday sun
From far-off Fairyland have run.
I had to run for I'm a Sprite,
A sort-of Fairy, but not quite;
And Sprites must run where Fairies fly.
Indeed that's why I'm here, to try
To win the wings of Fairyhood.
Well, Puss has done me one turn good
So further help from him I'll seek.
I'll give to him - Nay, I'll not speak.
'Tis safer I should prudent be
E'en though there's none to challenge me.

(MUSIC 17. BLUE SPOT UP L., and DEMON OLDBAD totters on. He is very aged and carries a small box and some matches.)

DEMON: That's where you're wrong, my pert young miss,
As you shall find when I've fix'd this.

(Gets painfully down on knees, puts small box in floats, lights a match and applies it to box. Very small blue flash.)

'Tis some time since I work'd that trick;
Remote control is much more slick,
But I can't quite recall the knack.
Not all my pow'rs though are so slack.

(Starts to rise with difficulty. SPRITE moves towards him.)

SPRITE: Oh, poor old man, I'll help thee rise.

DEMON: No, no, girl! Don't you realise
I am thy enemy most dread?

(Completes getting to his feet too sharply and clutches back in pain.)

Oh dear, my back!

(SPRITE moves to help him again. He brushes her aside.)

Let be, I said!
Why, soon I'll set such havoc free
'Twill ruin both thy charge and thee
And lose thee thy immortal life!
For always, howe'er hard the strife,
I, Demon Oldbad, get my Sprite! (is overcome by a paroxysm of coughing)
Oh, curse this cough!

(Claps hands. Old woollen shawl thrown on L., which he wraps round shoulders.)

SPRITE: It serves thee right!
And I'll thy boasting make thee rue
For I'm one Sprite ye'll ne'er subdue!
So, to my task on wingtips fleet.
Oh, bother no. On my two feet.

(Exit SPRITE R. WHITE SPOT OUT.)

DEMON: Ha! Serves her right, o'erweening miss!
Was youth always as young as this?
Nine thousand is too old to know.
I was retir'd some aeons ago,
But Demons are in short supply
So back to work they've call'd me, aye.
Oh dear! I have forgot what at.
Something was it about a cat?
Dick Whittington? No. Philip! Yes!
Now how'll I cause him most distress?
Ah, I'll his brothers turn 'gainst him,
They too the cat's nine lives shall trim.
Aha! they come. I'll stand aside
In other words - I'm going to hide.

I - 1 - 18

(Exit L. BLUE SPOT OUT, LIGHTS UP.)

PHIDDLE: (off in Mill) Left a bit. Right a bit. Ow! Mind out!

(Appears backwards through Mill door carrying one end of a brass and oak chest. PHADDLE holds the other end.)

Right, easy down the steps. I'll take the weight.

PHADDLE: Righto. (lets go of chest)

PHIDDLE: Hey! Not too fast! (stumbles backwards down steps to R.C. and falls with chest on top of himself.) OW! What are you doing up there? You should be at the other end.

PHADDLE: (moving down) Why? You said you'd take the weight.

PHIDDLE: Yes, but I - oh well. (rises) Let's look inside. (lifts lid) No. No, I daren't look. The sight of all that money would be too much for me. Tell me - how much is there?

PHADDLE: (bringing out coin) A penny.

PHIDDLE: A PENNY! One miserable penny! (snatches coin) That's not a penny, that's a golden guinea. Are you sure there aren't any more of these?

PHADDLE: No, but there's an old cloak. (takes out a red robe, trimmed with ermine) And a toy crown. (takes out a coronet)

PHIDDLE: (taking them) Well, we might be able to flog 'em. Is that the lot?

PHADDLE: (bringing out bag) No, there's a bag of glass beads.

PHIDDLE: (peering into bag) Glass beads! What's the use of - (digs hand into bag and brings some out) You nit! They're jewels! Diamonds! Rubies! Emeralds! We're rich! Rich!

PHADDLE: Philip is, you mean.

PHIDDLE: I'm not so sure about that. (replaces stones in bag and takes out will) How do we know he read this right? How do we know he's not cheating us? Oh, if only we could read.

DEMON: (peering on L.) Aha! This is my moment. (steps on) Sirs!

(PHIDDLE hastily throws robe and coronet into chest, snatches bag from PHADDLE and throws that in, then slams lid and sits on chest.)

                Oh, wait a bit. My mem'ry stirs.
                I now recall that little trick,
                It needs a sort of double flick. (makes involved hand passes towards floats)
                Like that. (pause) Or was it?
                (moves down to box)   Oh, dear, dear.

(BIG BLUE FLASH. DEMON retreats in alarm. PHIDDLE falls off chest and PHADDLE crouches behind it.)

PHADDLE: Hey, someone's launching rockets here.

I - 1 - 19

DEMON: Your pardon, sirs, but just before
I nearly set fire to the floor
I heard ye wish the pow'r to read.
Well, I can swift fulfil that need.

PHIDDLE: I don't believe it.

PHADDLE: Nor do I.

DEMON: Then let me prove it.

PHIDDLE: All right, try.

DEMON: (aside) I used to do this rather well,
My higher education spell.

(MUSIC 18. Does a little dance round them making elaborate magic passes during the following.)

Abracadabra and A B C.
Thy minds shall an open Sesame be,
With an M.A., B.A., B.Sc.,
Together with an A-level G.C.E.
(finishes triumphant but breathless.)

PHIDDLE: Well, what's the point of all that jazz?
That can't have done it.

PHADDLE: No.

BOTH: (looking at will) It has!

PHIDDLE: (feverishly searching will)
Now where's that bit? Ah! "Last bequest,
I leave the brass and oaken chest - (turns page)
To Philip". Ooh, the chiselling cuss!
He's told the truth and diddled us!

DEMON: Well, I can swiftly wrong that right,
Just see if this will mends thy plight.

(Produces will exactly like the other and gives it to PHIDDLE.)

PHADDLE: They look the same, the writing too.

DEMON: But not what's written.

PHIDDLE: Eh? Oh, coo!
This will leaves us the blooming lot
And Philip not one tiny jot!
Well, that's more like it.

PHADDLE: It's a fraud.

PHIDDLE: I know, but truth we can't afford.
(tears up 1st will)
Young Philip we shall have to ditch
And say our rights he tried to snitch
By doing of a naughty deed.
Viz - fibbing us 'cos we can't read.

PHIDDLE:	(continued) Which forces us to turn him out.
DEMON:	A pretty plan without a doubt.
PHADDLE:	But he might starve.
PHIDDLE:	He won't, you ninny, I'll stretch a point, give him the guinea.
PHADDLE:	Well, I won't help.
PHIDDLE:	Oh yes, you will, Or else to fishpaste in the Mill I shall your little guppies grind!
PHADDLE:	You wouldn't!
PHIDDLE:	Would! (aside to AUDIENCE) Not really, mind. (to PHADDLE) So you behave. (to DEMON) Well, ta-ta, mate, And thanks for this. (starts to go)
DEMON:	Delighted. Wait! (takes back will) There is a small return I'd ask.
PHIDDLE:	I knew it.
DEMON:	'Tis a simple task - To drown the Puss.
PHIDDLE:	Not quite my taste, But he won't mind.
PHADDLE:	I will!
PHIDDLE:	Fishpaste.
DEMON:	You'll do it, then, without delay?
PHIDDLE:	(pushing PHADDLE off before him into Mill and taking will) Of course, at once. Puss, Puss! Good-day.
DEMON:	Well, that's not strain'd my powers much, There's no doubt I've retain'd my touch. That Princess, my sun could cloud - Ah! I'll bewitch her, make her proud. 'Twill teach that silly Sprite to scoff. I'll show the Minx. (coughs) Oh, blow this cough.

(Exits L. PHADDLE enters from Mill with a bucket and a saucer of milk.)

PHADDLE: Ooh, Phiddle is rotten. (sighs) I hope this will be enough to drown him. (puts bucket down) Puss, Puss!

MIME PUSS: (entering L.) Miaow!

PHADDLE: (putting saucer down) I've got some milk for you. Puss, I thought you might like a last - I mean, I thought I'd give you something before I -

(MIME PUSS moves to PHADDLE and rubs head against his legs.)

PHADDLE: (continued) Oh dear. (bursts into tears)

(MIME PUSS starts to wash)

It's not my fault, Puss. I'm going to - to - Well, it's you or the guppies, and they've only got one life to your nine, so - You're not listening to a word I'm saying, are you? And you've not touched your milk.

(MIME PUSS shakes head and stalks L.)

It's for drinking. You know, lap-lap. Like this. (gets down on all fours and laps milk.) Ooh, rather nice.

(He continues lapping. PUSS regards him as if he is mad. PHIDDLE appears in Mill doorway, wearing a top hat adorned with large crepe mourning band and bow and covering his eyes with one hand.)

PHIDDLE: All over?

MIME PUSS: Miaow.

PHIDDLE: Was that his ghost? (cautiously uncovers eyes and sees PUSS and then PHADDLE) Phaddle, what are you playing at? I can see I'll have to do it myself. (removes topper and advances on PUSS) Come on, Puss, I'm going to give you a drink. A nice big drink.

(Grabs hold of PUSS and drags him to bucket. PUSS protests loudly when he sees PHIDDLE's intention. Excited ad libs from PHIDDLE and PHADDLE. NEDDY runs on R. to see what all the commotion is about and tries to stop it.)

Neddy, go away! I'll saddle you, if you're not careful.

(NEDDY kicks him and runs off L., braying loudly.)

PHIDDLE: Ouch!

(CHORUS run on L. and R. shouting "What's the matter", etc. MARY runs on backwards R. and collides with some of them.)

MARY: Sorry, but you weren't looking where I was going.

PHILIP: (off L.) Yes, all right, Neddy. but what's the matter? (enters L. with PRINCESS) What's all the - Phiddle! Stop that! Let go! (grabs hold of him) D'you hear? Let go!

(EFFECTS 14. GLASS CRASH off L. ROWLEY runs on L.)

ROWLEY: Look out! Here come the King and Queen again! (stopping D.R.) Ooh, silver bells on a plant. I think I'll take one.

(Puts out hand. EFFECTS 15. BELLS JINGLE. AUDIENCE shout. ROWLEY jumps away from plant. JIMOTHY runs on R.)

JIMOTHY: Thank you. I say, what's going on here?

(KING, with a lampost over his head, and QUEEN enter L.)

QUEEN: Goodness gracious, what a commotion!

(PHIDDLE releases PUSS and commotion stops.)

QUEEN: (continued) Now what seems to be the trouble?

(Everyone starts talking at once.)

One at a time, please!

PHIDDLE: It was a little dispute over this chest, your Majesty. (takes out will)

PHILIP: The chest? What are you talking about?

PHIDDLE: My brother Philip here says our old dad left it to him in this will, but we think he meant us to have it. But we can't read so we don't know whether he's telling fibs or not.

QUEEN: Then your King shall settle the matter. (takes will and gives it to KING) Marmaduke, who's been left the chest? I should remove that lampost first.

KING: (doing so) Thought it might throw a little light on the - er - Well, it says - er - leave the brass and oaken chest to - er - yes. (hands will back)

QUEEN: To whom, Marmaduke?

KING: I just - er - Phiddle and Phaddle.

PHIDDLE: There, he did try to cheat us!

(Cries of "Shame! Liar!" etc.)

PHILIP: But I didn't! I didn't!

(Cries of "You did! Thief!" etc.)

Doesn't anybody believe me? Esmerelda!

(PRINCESS opens her mouth to speak and the DEMON appears behind her. MUSIC TING as he makes magic pass over her head.)

PRINCESS: Kindly don't speak to me, young man. I never converse with commoners.

(Sweeps off L. DEMON follows her, chuckling softly and rubbing hands with glee.)

PHILIP: Princess!

(MIME PUSS gently rubs head against PHILIP's legs. Cries of "Turn him out" etc.)

PHIDDLE: Oh no, I couldn't, I couldn't.

PHILIP: Don't worry. I'm going.

MIME PUSS: (points to himself) Miaow.

PHILIP: You want to come with me? Thank you, Puss.

PHADDLE: Wait! (to PHIDDLE) The guinea! You said you'd give him the guinea!

I - 1 - 23

PHIDDLE: I wish you'd belt up. I might have saved it. Oh well. Here, Philip, take this, it's all the money father left! (presses guinea into PHILIP's hand)

PHILIP: I don't want it. I don't want anything. (throws it down)

(MIME PUSS shakes head and moves to take it.)

No, come on, Puss, we'll manage without it.

(Exits R. MIME PUSS hesitates a moment then picks it up and follows PHILIP.)

QUEEN: Well, now we can turn to more pleasant matters. Tell them about the levee tomorrow, Marmaduke.

KING: Very well. With the coming of age of our - er - we shall hold a - for all suitable - er - and as the Ogre ate up all last year's - er - the one with the most - er - will win the hand of our - er - all clear?

QUEEN: Abundantly. All suitable suitors. The Palace. Three p.m. sharp tomorrow.

PHIDDLE: Suitable suitors? That's us!

CH BOYS: And us!

ROWLEY: And me.

QUEEN: Well, everybody come and we'll sort you out there. It'll be quite a celebration. So let's practice celebrating now.

<u>MUSIC 19. "MARMALADIA"</u>

ALL:
It's holiday in Marmaladia,
As announced on our local radia.
Let's all go madly gay, dear.
Let's go out and play.
Let us spend Marmaladian money.
Let's have fun while the weather is sunny.
Happy folk of Marmaladia,
Shout, "Hip-hip-hooray!"
For our public holiday.

(BLACKOUT.

Close traverse tabs. Fly in frontcloth.)

Scene Two - A WOODLAND GLADE

(Tabs to begin, woodland cloth with rabbit burrows painted in C. (3 of the holes practical), revealed later. Clump of dandelions set L. DEMON's SPOT comes up L. Slight pause and DEMON peers on L. looking testily at flash box in floats.)

DEMON: Oh, come on, do! (makes a few agitated passes at it)
No, all in vain. (enters fully)
The wretched thing's misfired again
My other magic's gone so well,
Especially my proud-making spell;
It quite transform'd that sweet Princess
The cat's disposal lack'd success,
But still, I've cause enough for glee,
Even my cough's not troubling me -
I exercised it with some Vic!

(Starts to exit chuckling, stops to try a hopeful pass or two at flash box then shrugs and moves off.)

Oh, dash, what was that double flick?

(Exit L. BLUE SPOT OUT. MUSIC 20. SPRITE's SPOT UP R.)

SPRITE: (off R.) Hurry, Youngood, you're late, I vow.

(Runs on R., rather breathless again, disguised with a false nose, moustache and glasses and wearing a cap and a cobbler's leather apron. Her little wand is behind her ear and she carries a stool, a hammer, an old shoe and a bag containing the boots.)

Well, never mind, I've got here now.
Hullo, it's me, I'm in disguise,
I thought 'twould take you by surprise.

(BLUE FLASH L. SPRITE jumps in alarm.)

Help! That took me. How very queer,
But still it show's just who's been here.
My work then must be extra good.
Now I'm a cobbler -

(MUSIC 21. Indicates to tabs to open, which they do and sits on stool. (If a cloth is not used open tabs only sufficiently to show a flat - a 6ft would be ample with the rabbit burrows in a woodland setting.)

In a wood.
A most unlikely thing, I know,
But why I'm here I soon will show.
I hope. I'm trembling to the core -
I've never work'd a spell before!

(Sets to work holding the old shoe on her knee and tapping it with hammer. PUSS enters L., beckoning to urge on PHILIP, who follows, tired and disspirited.)

PHILIP: Yes, coming, Puss. But, oh dear me.

I - 2 - 25

PHILIP: (continued)
> I seem so very tir'd to be,
> My feet ache -

(PUSS looks at own feet and agrees. SPRITE tries to draw attention to herself by tapping louder.)

> But my heart aches more.
> All turn'd against us, but what for?
> And why cast out like broken toys?

(SPRITE taps harder still.)

> I say, who's making all this noise?

(They turn and see SPRITE.)

SPRITE: (in disguised voice) The cobbler in the wood am I,
Most expert in the craft I ply,
Each nail I hit with eye so true. (hits thumb and cries out)

PHILIP: I fear you hit your thumbnail too.

SPRITE: (sucking thumb) A hazard of the trade, fine sir,
Such things good cobblers don't deter.
But what's for you? A sole and heel?
Or p'raps some new boots would appeal?

(Takes red boots out of bag. PUSS is immediately interested in them.)

PHILIP: Too small.

PUSS: (points to himself) Miaow.

PHILIP: For you?

(PUSS nods.)

> But what's the good?
> Cats don't wear boots.

SPRITE: Well then, they should.
And at one guinea, they're not dear.

PHILIP: We haven't got that much, I fear.

(PUSS nudges PHILIP and holds out the guinea in a paw.)

> What's that? A guinea! But, Puss, where -

(PUSS looks around airily, disinclined to discuss the matter.)

> Ah, wait, of course. Puss, that's not fair.
> You know I threw that money back
> And I'll not touch it now.

(PUSS shrugs testily indicating his disinterest in such petty scruples.)

SPRITE: Alack!
I have my living sir to make.
A wife. Six kids!

PHILIP: We-ll - for your sake.

SPRITE: Thank you.

(PUSS points to bag.)

> Yes, take the bag as well.

(PUSS hands SPRITE money and takes bag.)

> (taking wand from behind ear. Aside)
> And now here goes then with that spell.

(Two MUSIC tings as she marks sole of each boot with wand. She gives boots to PUSS.)

> You'll find these will good care repay.

(PUSS nods wisely.)

> (gathering stool etc.)
> Now I'll be off. Goodbye.

PHILIP: Good-day.

(SPRITE exits R. PUSS lovingly examines the boots, looks at the place SPRITE marked them and nods head wisely.)

> Well, Puss, you've got your boots. (yawns)
> I think I'll have a little rest. (sits down
> wearily L., facing away from PUSS.)
> But I'm sure they're not going to be any use
> to you. (yawns again and starts to fall asleep)

(PUSS looks at him quizzically for a moment then puts a foot into one boot. BLACKOUT. WHITE FLASH. Cymbal roll. MIME PUSS exits. TALKING PUSS enters. LIGHTS UP. PUSS is revealed standing on his hind legs with his boots on in a skin tight costume and a mask that shows most of the face, also a little red coat and a red hat. SPRITE, as herself, pops her head on R., excitedly.)

SPRITE: Whoopee - I've work'd it! My first spell!
Bravo, wand! You've done jolly well!
At this rate very soon we'll see
My Fairy wings a-sprouting. Wheeee!

(Disappears. PUSS smiles and raises hat to her as she goes.)

PUSS: Indeed, well done. A perfect fit.

PHILIP: (drowsily) What are?

PUSS: My boots, of course, master.

PHILIP: Oh, your boots, Puss. (suddenly sits up wide-eyed) What! No. He couldn't have. I must have dreamt it.

PUSS: Oh no, master.

PHILIP: (turning in astonishment) Puss! You - you did talk! But how? You've never talked before.

PUSS: I've never had boots before.

PHILIP: You mean you can talk when you wear boots?

PUSS: We-ll, these boots. But let's not waste time, master. We must set about making your fortune. As your first step on the road to fame, pick me some dandelion leaves. (points to them.)

PHILIP: Do what?

PUSS: Don't look so puzzled. Everything will be all right if you do as I say and leave the thinking to me, - master.

PHILIP: It seems to me you're more the master.

PUSS: Oh no. You're the master - master. (gets down on all fours and rubs head against PHILIP's legs) Miaow! (looking up into PHILIP's face) Please pick some dandelion leaves, Master.

PHILIP: (laughs) All right. (moves to pick dandelion leaves L.) What are they for, though?

PUSS: Bait. We're going hunting. (picks up bag) I knew this bag would come in useful. (crouches beside the holes in C. of cloth, holding the bag under 1st hole (numbered from R.)) Now, put some of the leaves in front of each hole.

(PHILIP does so.)

Now watch.

(MUSIC 22. A rabbit pops out of the 1st hole and falls into the bag. PUSS clasps the neck of the bag together and moves to 2nd hole. The process is repeated here and then at the 3rd hole. PUSS pulls the strings tight at the top of the bag and rises.)

There!

PHILIP: Very neat. But surely one rabbit would have been enough to feed us.

PUSS: Oh, they're not for us. They're for the King. I'll take them to the Palace tomorrow. A little present of game from the estates of the Marquess of Carabas.

PHILIP: What are you talking about?

PUSS: You. From now on you're the Marquess of Carabas.

PHILIP: But that's ridiculous. Nobody would believe I was a Marquess.

PUSS: I quite agree, I shall deal with the little matter of making you look like a Marquess later.

PHILIP: Puss, I don't like the idea. It's a deliberate deception.

PUSS: Is it? Let's say invention, master. Or rather, re-invention. I've reinvented you as the Marquess of Carabas.

PHILIP: But why?

PUSS: Bless me, what a man you are for questions. Because you're in love with the Princess of course. But she won't have anything to do with you as you are now, will she?

PHILIP: You needn't rub it in.

PUSS: Don't lose heart. She will. With your looks and my brains we'll win through. But chiefly with my brains.

(Close traverse tabs slowly during number. Fly out cloth on strike flat.)

MUSIC 23. "WE'RE A TEAM!"

PUSS:
With your sort of looks
From picture books,
And then again,
My sort of brain
We can get right on the beam.

BOTH: Shake, partner! We're a team!

PHILIP:
Since you have some wit
And I'm a hit,
It is agreed
We can succeed
Far beyond our wildest dream

BOTH: Shake, partner! We're a team!

PUSS:
Let's turn on the tap.
You are Homo Sap.
I am very feline

PHILIP:
We need never stop
For the very top
Let us make a beeline.

BOTH:
We together are
Travelling far,
And we have got
Almost the lot!

PUSS: And I like my cream with cream!
BOTH: Shake partner! We're a team!

(BLACKOUT.

Open traverse tabs.)

Scene Three - THE AUDIENCE CHAMBER AT THE PALACE

(Full set. Cut-out ground-row of row of pillars on front of rostrum. Wings L. and R. U.L.C., angled onstage, a small dais with double throne on it, covered with a dust sheet. Sceptre and orb set on throne. Gilt and plush chair to L. of throne. Enter QUEEN L., wearing large apron, dust sleeves, and a mob cap underneath her crown. She is busy with a list and pencil. EFFECTS 16. A clock chimes a half-hour off as she enters.)

QUEEN: Good gracious, half-past two and not an ashtray emptied. (to AUDIENCE) Ah, still nightime in your part of the world, I see. We're in rather a rush to get ready for the levee so you will excuse me if I go on with the housework. In Marmaladia the Royal Family always does its own housework; we're very democratic, you know - also we're skint. Now where was I? (consults list) Ah, clean Audience Chamber. I told the Court Chamberlain to see to that, I wonder where he's got to. Lord Snoozle! Where are you?

(A snore from under dust-sheet on throne.)

Ah, that sounded like his voice. We have a bit of trouble keeping him awake because he was the Chamberlain at the court of the Sleeping Beauty for some little time - over a hundred years, in fact. I don't think he's quite got over it.

(Louder snore. She moves up looking.)

Well, he must be here somewhere. Lord Snoozle! Wake up, Snoozle! It's half-past twoozle! (moves round behind throne)

(As she does so, LORD SNOOZLE rises under dust-sheet, stretching his arms wide in a yawn. QUEEN comes from behind throne on L. side.)

Not there. Well, where can he - (sees the ghostly figure) Waaaah! (faints into chair)

(SNOOZLE emerges from dust-sheet. He wears a Chamberlain's robe over a nightshirt, with bedsocks and a nightcap.

SNOOZLE: (very sleepy and yawny) Did someone call? Oh, Your Majesty - why, bless my sheets and pillowcases, she's gone to sleep. Very sensible. I'll go and do the same. (carelessly throws dust-sheet over QUEEN and wanders yawning and blinking R.) Hm, little silver bells growing on a plant. Well, I need a new bell for my alarm clock, I'll take one.

(Moves to do so. EFFECTS 17. BELLS JINGLE. AUDIENCE shout. SNOOZLE jumps back very alarmed and wideawake. JIMOTHY runs on L., in shirtsleeves and green baize apron, carrying two buckets, two brooms, some dusters and a prop floor polisher fitted with castors.)

JIMOTHY: Thank you. Lord Snoozle, I'm surprised at you, that's my silver bell plant.

SNOOZLE: Well, bless my alarums and excursions, you're welcome to it. Nothing's woken me up so much for years. I'll probably have to

I - 3 - 30

SNOOZLE: (continued) take a sleeping pill to get off to sleep at all.
(exits R.)

JIMOTHY: (calling after him) But what about all these things? Aren't you going to clean out the room?

(Moans from QUEEN as she starts to recover.)

Ooh, what was that? It sounded like a ghost. But that's silly. This room's not haunted.

(Turns and sees QUEEN rising covered by sheet and still moaning. He drops buckets etc., with a clatter, which makes the QUEEN give a startled cry and raise her hands under the sheet before collapsing again into chair.)

(running off R.) Aah! Help! (exits)

KING: (off L.) Queenie, Queenie, where are -

(Enters L. tugging at a vacuum cleaner hose and wearing a little frilly apron with a feather duster stuck in the waistband and a knotted handkerchief underneath crown.)

Oh, not - er - never mind, I'll just whisk round here with the - er - seems to have got - er -

(Gives hose a tug and pulls on large prop cylinder type vacuum cleaner, fitted with little wheels on which SNOOZLE sits fast asleep.)

Ah, that ex - er - it's Snoozled.

(Turns as QUEEN moans and starts to rise.)

Oh - er - ooh. (backing to L.) I think I'm going to - er - bit hard here, though - er - find somewhere where it's - er - (stumbles off L.) Ah, first grade Wilton, deli - Oooh.

(EFFECTS 18. Thud offstage as he subsides. QUEEN moves R. trying to get out of sheet and clatters about among buckets which wakes SNOOZLE, who looks up sleepily and falls off cleaner.)

SNOOZLE: (feebly) Help! I've just seen - too much cheese for supper!

(Staggers to his feet and QUEEN, in her efforts to get clear moves toward him. SNOOZLE backs U.L.)

Help! I'm - Ooh. (faints behind throne)

QUEEN: (managing to struggle out of sheet) How did I get under this? (throws it behind throne)

(KING and JIMOTHY creep on L. and R., looking fearfully around, to either side of QUEEN.)

There's something spooky going on here.

KING & JIM: (in sibilant whisper) Pssst!

QUEEN: (twirls round in fright) Aah! Oh, it's you two. I thought it was a ghost.

KING: A ghost? (trying to laugh it off) Oh, come, come, Queenie, mustn't let your imagination run away with - er -

(SNOOZLE comes crawling slowly on all fours from behind R. side of throne with sheet draped over him.)

Me!

(SNOOZLE starts to rise with his back to them and all fall in a heap. He turns and sees them.)

SNOOZLE: Well, bless my slippers and bedsocks, now they've all gone to sleep. Tut, tut, someone's been mucking around with a spinning wheel again, I suppose. I'd better get back to bed if I'm in for another hundred years.

(Exits R. OTHERS recover and sit up.)

QUEEN: What a terrible experience. I hope we see no more nasty apparitions like that.

(Enter ROWLEY R. as they rise. He carries a grip and wears combinations and a hat which he doffs.)

(hastily hiding eyes) Ooh!

(JIMOTHY whips out a handkerchief and holds it up in front of ROWLEY.

ROWLEY: Hullo, I'm a sui - sui - Achoo!

JIMOTHY: A suisuiachoo? What's that?

ROWLEY: No, a suitor. I sneezed.

JIMOTHY: I'm not surprised, dressed like that.

ROWLEY: Oh, I've brought my other clothes with me. But my mother said if I wanted to be a suitor I'd have to press my suit here. (takes iron out of grip)

(Enter MARY backwards L., carrying a vase with some flowers upside down in it. She cannons into group and turns.)

MARY: Ah, your Majesties, I thought you'd bump into me soon. I've arranged the flowers. How do you like them?

JIMOTHY: Aren't they just a teeny-weeny bit upside down?

MARY: No, they're completely upside down. They keep much fresher that way. Where shall I put them?

KING: Er -

QUEEN: Marmaduke! In the entrance hall, my dear, and then you can give us a hand to clean this room.

MARY: Righto. (exits backwards R.)

QUEEN: As you're a little early, Mr Rowley, you can help too by giving the throne a dust.

(JIMOTHY gives ROWLEY a duster. MISTRESS MARY re-enters backwards R. with a mop and a bucket of water. She dips mop in bucket,

(squeezes it out, puts bucket off, turns mop upside down and vigorously mops floor with the handle end. All watch her as she crosses stage and exits L.)

QUEEN: Well, I suppose it saves getting the floor wet. I'll get on with the Hoovering. (moves to vacuum and calls off) Mary, would you plug this into the mains, please?

MARY: (off L.) Righto.

QUEEN: You do the floor polishing, Jimothy, and, Marmaduke, you have a go at the cobwebs.

(ROWLEY starts to dust throne. JIMOTHY starts using floor polisher. KING leaps about stage reaching for cobwebs with his feather duster.)

Ah, what a loss you are to the royal ballet, Marmaduke.

(JIMOTHY decides he could get along quicker by using the polisher as a scooter.)

And I take it we shall be seeing you on ice soon, Jimothy.

(Enter MARY L.)

MARY: I've plugged in. Shall I switch on?

QUEEN: Please, dear. (holds nozzle to ground)

(MARY operates switch on machine.)

Nothing seems to be happening.

(Lifts hose as she turns to talk so that nozzle points at ROWLEY's behind as he bends over working at throne.)

Are you sure you plugged it into the Mains?

MARY: Yes, quite sure.

(A jet of water shoots out of nozzle onto ROWLEY's behind. He jumps up clutching himself.)

QUEEN: Must have been the water mains.

ROWLEY: (holding coms away from himself with legs apart) Oh dear, what am I going to tell Mother?

JIMOTHY: Just say you had a little accident. No, perhaps not.

QUEEN: (handing him his iron) You can iron out your troubles, dear boy. Then you need only say you were pressed in the extreme.

(ROWLEY takes iron, picks up grip and exits unhappily L. **EFFECT 19.** Clock striking three.)

JIMOTHY: Blimey! Three o'clock!

QUEEN: The suitors!

KING: The - er - yes!

QUEEN: Quick, help us to get ready, dears.

I - 3 - 33

(KING pushes cleaner off L. MARY helps QUEEN out of apron, etc., and JIMOTHY helps KING as SNOOZLE enters R., carrying wand of office. He bangs on floor with it.)

SNOOZLE: (yawns) The court is assembled and her Highness's suitors are here, your Majesties. (yawns again, bows and nods off to sleep leaning on staff.)

(MUSIC 24. CHORUS as courtiers enter R. and process round stage, rather hampered by the buckets and brooms, etc., which JIMOTHY is collecting.)

JIMOTHY: Excuse me. Sorry, etc.

(MARY hurries off backwards L. with the KING and QUEEN's aprons etc. JIMOTHY exits R. with cleaning things except one broom. Procession ends with CHORUS bowing and curtseying to KING and QUEEN. QUEEN sits on throne covering sceptre.)

KING: (sits on orb) Ouch! (picks it up and sits with it in one hand and the feather duster in the other)

QUEEN: (out of side of mouth) The sceptre, Marmaduke, not the feather duster.

KING: What? Oh, yes - er - (tosses it behind throne and searches for sceptre.)

QUEEN: Well, we're delighted -

(KING finds sceptre and tries to tug it from underneath her.

Marmaduke! Oh, I see. As I was saying, we're delighted to welcome you.

(Loud snore from SNOOZLE.)

Yes, what is it, Snoozle?

SNOOZLE: (still asleep) Her Royal Highness, the Princess Esmerelda. (bangs three times with wand, hitting his own foot on the third bang and waking) Ow! (drops off to sleep again)

(MUSIC 25. CHORUS bow and curtsey as MARY enters backwards L., holding ESMERELDA's train and pulling her on backwards.)

PRINCESS: This hardly seems very dignified, Mary.

QUEEN: Ah, Esmerelda, my dear. Pray be seated.

(PRINCESS sits on chair, MARY positions herself behind it.)

Let the suitors present themselves.

(PHIDDLE and PHADDLE arrive R., rather ridiculously smartened up.)

PHIDDLE: (to SNOOZLE) Oi, shop!

SNOOZLE: (wakes) What?

(PHIDDLE hands him huge visiting card.)

Well, bless my pasteboard and printing. Er-hm, Messrs. Phiddle and Phaddle.

PHADDLE: We're not messers. We're very smart. We got all specially dolled up for this.

PHIDDLE: Ssh, leave the talking to me, just do what I do.

(Enter JIMOTHY R.)

JIMOTHY: Excuse me, I want to get -

PHIDDLE: 'Ere, 'ere, 'ere, you wait your turn. (advances to throne with one hand outstretched and doffing hat with other) How de do, your - (trips and falls flat over remaining broom)

JIMOTHY: That's what I wanted to get. (moves to take it.)

PHADDLE: Hey, don't take it yet, I've got to do what he did. (moving forward to throne as PHIDDLE did) How de do, your - (trips and falls flat beside PHIDDLE) All right?

PHIDDLE: No.

(JIMOTHY shrugs, picks up broom and exits R.)

QUEEN: Are you two gentlemen suitors?

PHIDDLE: (rising) Oh yes, your Queenship, we're suitors. (hissing at PHADDLE) Get up.

(PHADDLE rises.)

(bowing) Aha, I can see her ducky little Highness fancies me already.

(Bestows large wink on her, she turns away very aloof.)

And I don't think you could do much better than one of us. We've got the looks and the lolly.

QUEEN: Lolly? How much?

PHIDDLE: Well, we're not sure at the moment. It's all in jewels.

KING: Jew - er - oh, ah! Still, I suppose we'll have to see all the - er - any more?

CH BOYS: (stepping forward and bowing) Yes, your Majesty.

(ROWLEY runs on L., now dressed.)

ROWLEY: And me! Sorry I'm late, I've been having a bit of trouble trying to get into my coms. (holds out miniature coms.) They've shrunk.

KING: Never mind, we won't let that disquali - er - so now we can de - er - can't we?

PRINCESS: No, father, we can't. There are no noblemen here. As a Princess I insist on marrying someone of noble birth.

QUEEN: But, Esmerelda, you've never worried about such things before.

PRINCESS: I know. It seemed to strike me suddenly yesterday. I feel I must marry a Marquess at the very least.

QUEEN: A Marquess? But we don't know any Marquesses.

(Enter JIMOTHY L., scratching his head rather puzzled.)

JIMOTHY: Your Majesties, a - er - a "messenger" from the Marquess of Carabas is outside.

KING & QUEEN:	From the Marquess of Carabas?
OTHERS:	The Marquess of Carabas?
PRINCESS:	The Marquess of Carabas! How marvellous!
KING & QUEEN:	How opportune!
CH GIRLS & MARY:	How intriguing!
CH BOYS, ROWLEY, PHIDDLE & PHADDLE:	How annoying!
QUEEN:	Admit this person instantly!
JIMOTHY:	He's not a person.
KING, QUEEN & PRINCESS:	Not a person?
OTHERS:	Not a person?

(The following should be done very rhythmically. A light percussion accompaniment could be used to advantage.)

JIMOTHY:	No. He's a sort of a, kind of a, well, he's a cat. But more than that, he's a talking cat.
KING, QUEEN & PRINCESS:	A talking cat?
MARY, ROW, PHI & PHA:	A talking cat?
ALL:	A TALKING CAT?
JIMOTHY:	A talking cat. And a nicely spoken talking cat.
ALL:	But a talking cat, a talking cat, Whoever heard of a thing like that?
KING:	It seems to me that it's sort of - well - I doubt it, but you never can tell.
QUEEN:	A dog or a horse -
PRINCESS:	Might speak, of course -
BOTH:	Or even a mouse or a shrew.
PHIDDLE:	And it wouldn't seem queer -
PHADDLE:	For a sheep or deer -
BOTH:	To utter a word or two.
MARY:	But cats never speak -

ROWLEY: They only squeak -
BOTH: And sometimes purr and mew.
SNOOZLE: (waking) Well, bless my lobes and eardrums too,
A talking cat, did I hear true?
ALL: Yes, a talking cat, a talking cat.
CHORUS: It's hard to believe in a thing like that.
Now if he'd said a fox or a rat
We wouldn't have been surprised.
But a talking cat, a talking cat -
PHADDLE: Perhaps it's a cow disguised?
JIMOTHY: No, no, it's a cat, it's a cat, it's a cat!
ALL: It can't be a cat, it can't be a cat.
JIMOTHY: It is a cat.
ALL: It can't be a cat.
JIMOTHY: It is a cat.
ALL: It can't be a cat.
JIMOTHY: It is.
ALL: BUT - CATS - CAN'T - TALK!

(PUSS enters R. and comes C., carrying his bag of rabbits.)

PUSS: Well, I can.
ALL: OOH!

MUSIC 26. "TALKING CAT"

PUSS: Natter, natter, natter, natter!
Your suggestions do not flatter.
Won't you even give a cat a
   Chance to say a word?
Since we never advertise
That cats can really vocalise
You're sitting up in great surprise
   And giving me the bird!

ALL: True we never realise
That cats of any shape and size
Would take an elocution prize -
   It seems to us absurd!

PUSS: You will find, on the contrary,
Some accommodating fairy
Gave us a vocabulary
   Larger far than most.
Though my grammar's rather wonky,
Though I'm singing in the wrong key,
I'd talk the hind leg off a donkey -
   And I never boast!

ALL:	Though he is of charm the essence, Though he seems to have some dress-sense, We're inclined to doubt his presence - Have we seen a ghost?

PUSS:	Right across the feline nation
	I've achieved a reputation
	For amusing conversation -
	    That is "comme il faut".
	That is why, when I'm employing
	Words that others are enjoying
	It is really most annoying
	    You don't want to know.

ALL:	We admit it is amazing. Dutifully we are praising Such a rhetorical phrasing! Have another go!

PUSS:	With intellect empirical
	Loquacity so lyrical
	It's not at all a miracle
	    Not by the longest chalk.
	Your ideas are all out of date.
	I hope you now appreciate
	    That CATS CAN TALK!

ALL:	Goodness, goodness, gracious! In this age atomic spacious, CATS CAN TALK!
KING:	Well, I'm abso - er - flabber - stounded.
PUSS:	(bows) Your Majesty, my master the Marquess of Carabas, begs leave to present his humble loyalty to yourself and trusts you will accept this trifling gift of game from his estates. (bows again and gives KING bag.)
KING:	Oh, rabbits. How de - especially cooked in - er - and served with - er - aren't they, my love?
QUEEN:	Yes, indeed, Marmaduke, and what splendidly plump rabbits. Has the Marquess large estates?
PUSS:	Vast, ma'am, vast.
QUEEN:	Really? He must be very rich then.
PUSS:	His wealth is so great that it bores him, your Majesty.
QUEEN:	I just love that kind of boredom.
PHIDDLE:	There must be something wrong with him. I bet he's ugly.
PUSS:	Well, sir, if you are handsome, then the Marquess is indeed ugly. My master has heard many tales of the Princess's beauty - and I see they are not idle tales, if I may venture so far - (bows to PRINCESS) and these have prompted him to send me to ask if he may

PUSS: (continued) presume to be considered as a suitor for her Highness's exquisite hand.

PRINCESS: Oh yes!

KING: Delight - er -

QUEEN: Definitely! And the sooner we meet this delicious Marquess the better. We're having a picnic by the lake tomorrow, perhaps the Marquess would care to join us.

PUSS: (to himself) By the lake? Yes! (to them) I shall prevail on my master to make every endeavour, ma'am.

QUEEN: Splendid! Isn't that splendid, Marmaduke? I'm sure any man who has such an intelligent talking cat must be very worth meeting.

PUSS: He is indeed, your Majesty.

MUSIC 27. "TALKING CAT" (Reprise)

> Soon my master you will see
> And then I'm sure you will agree
> He's quite as nice a chap as me -
> You should enjoy your walk!
> In such funny days as these
> The moon is made of cheddar cheese
> And choc'late biscuits grow on trees
> And CATS CAN TALK!

ALL: It is our good fortune
We can sing the words of your tune -
Natter, natter, natter, natter
Natter, natter, natter, natter!
CATS CAN TALK!
Miaow!

(BLACKOUT.

Close traverse tabs, fly in frontcloth.

Music continues into next scene.)

Scene Four - A STREET OUTSIDE THE PALACE

(Tabs or frontcloth. If cloth is used open tabs when ready during scene. As lights go up PUSS skips on L., still singing, highly delighted with himself.)

PUSS: Nothing could be cuter
Than a cat as proxy suitor
Hooray, hooray, hooray, hooray,
Hooray, hooray, hooray, hooray!
I can talk!

(PHILIP enters R.)

PUSS: Master, your fortunes are as good as made. And tomorrow - tomorrow, they will be made.

PHILIP: What do we do today then?

PUSS: We live for tomorrow.

PHILIP: And when do we eat? I'm jolly hungry.

PUSS: Oh, we shall certainly eat tomorrow. I've arranged for us to go on a picnic.

PHILIP: A picnic? Puss, I wish you'd tell me what you've been up to.

PUSS: I will, to -

PHILIP: Yes, I know, tomorrow.

PUSS: Exactly, tomorrow. After you, Master, lead on - to tomorrow.

(MUSIC 28. They exit R. DEMON'S SPOT UP L. He peers on.)

DEMON: I say, I think I've got it right.
(indicates L. end of floats)
You watch that spot, I'll leap in sight.
(withdraws head)
Stand by. (leaps on, assuming triumphant pose)

(BLUE FLASH R.)

Aha!
(stamping foot) Oh no! Ooh, dear!
(hops about, nursing foot)
Right on my favourite corn, I fear.
I've come here to disguise myself,
In order to forestall that elf;
For she'll soon try from Philip's kin
The contents of that chest to win!
But I'll be first and snatch the prize.
'Twon't cost a lot, for in my guise
I'll -

MUSIC 29.

DEMON: (continued)
Soft! She comes! Then I must go.
Don't worry, soon my ruse you'll know.

(Exit L. BLUE SPOT OUT. WHITE SPOT UP R. Enter SPRITE R.)

SPRITE: Well, so far since I cast my spell
I'm glad to say all's turn'd out well.
Now Philip's fortunes to ensure
I must that lost bequest secure,
So with his brothers twain I'll vie
And hope their price is not too high.
To buy it cheaply, shall be -
But here they come. Just wait, you'll see.

(Exit SPRITE R. Enter L. PHIDDLE and PHADDLE. PHIDDLE carrying bag of jewels, PHADDLE coronet and robes.)

PHIDDLE: Rabbits! Here we are, loaded with jewels, and all that Princess is interested in is a bloke what sends her Dad rabbits. I ask you, which would you rather have, jewels or rabbits?

PHADDLE: Rabbits.

PHIDDLE: You would.

PHADDLE: I should like a bunny - a mummy bunny with lots of little baby bunnies.

PHIDDLE: Mummy bunny! Don't you know the proper name for a mummy bunny.

PHADDLE: Yes. A mummy bunny.

PHIDDLE: No.

PHADDLE: No?

PHIDDLE: No. Doe.

PHADDLE: Have you caught a cold suddenly?

PHIDDLE: No. That's what a mummy bunny is. A doe.

PHADDLE: What's a daddy bunny then - a yes?

PHIDDLE: Doe. I mean, no. A daddy bunny's a buck. Surely you've heard of a buck rabbit?

PHADDLE: Yes, it's a Welsh Rabbit with a poached egg on top. I don't know how they keep them on though, running up and down all those mountains.

PHIDDLE: Not that kind of a - oh, never mind. Now where are we going to flog these things?

(Enter SPRITE R. and DEMON L., both in identical long cloaks and hats from the crowns of which rise pawnbrokers three ball signs. Both are also disguised with long beards and carry trays suspended from their necks, which have a few trinkets on them and notices hanging down in front, one of which reads - S. YOUNGOOD. ITINERANT PAWNBROKER.

(And the other – D. OLDBAD. ITINERANT PAWNBROKER.)

BOTH: (in assumed voices)
Any old ermine, gems, old gold?
Inheritances bought and sold!

(They take on each other. PHIDDLE and PHADDLE take on them each separately and then look back to one another.)

SPRITE: (in own voice) You copycat!

DEMON: (in own voice) You thieving shrew!
You've pinch'd my notion!

SPRITE: Sucks to you!
It's you who's stolen my idea!

PHADDLE: I think there's something funny here.

PHIDDLE: Professional jealousy I'd say.
But which d'you think the most will pay?

DEMON: (drawing them aside. In assumed voice)
You come to me, he'll do you down.
What have you?

PHIDDLE: Jewels.

PHADDLE: (giving cloak and coronet to DEMON) A cloak and crown.

DEMON: (examining cloak) Ah, rabbit dyed.
(examines crown) Best gilded brass.
(puts jeweller's eye-piece in eye and examines a few stones with other eye) And these – the very finest glass.
I'll gen'rous be, a pound the lot.

PHADDLE: See? Imitation.

PHIDDLE: No, they're not.

SPRITE: Dear gents, let me look, he's a fraud.

(PHIDDLE takes things from DEMON and passes them to SPRITE.)

This rabbit? Ermine, be assur'd.
And this pure gold, and these quite real
I know they are, just by the feel.
Oh, gents, he tried to diddle you.

(PHIDDLE and PHADDLE turn to look at DEMON and SPRITE pokes a long nose at him.)

PHIDDLE: One pound the lot, eh?

DEMON: Make it two.

(PHIDDLE turns away.)

Well, well, I'll make it guineas then.

PHIDDLE: And what's your price?

SPRITE:	Well, gentlemen, The market for these things is bad.
PHADDLE:	It always is.
SPRITE:	I know, it's sad. Still, just for you, a hundred pound.
PHIDDLE:	A hundred? That's a better sound.
DEMON:	I was just joking you before - Two hundred!
SPRITE:	Three!
PHIDDLE:	(rubbing hands) Ah, any more?
DEMON:	Four hundred!
SPRITE:	Five!
DEMON:	Six!
SPRITE:	Seven!
PHADDLE:	EIGHT!
PHIDDLE, DEMON & SPRITE:	What's that?
PHADDLE:	Oh, sorry.
PHIDDLE:	(to DEMON) Your turn, mate.
DEMON:	Eight hundred, then.

(PHIDDLE turns to SPRITE.)

And ninety nine!
(aside) And that is cutting it too fine,
Nine hundred and I'm up the spout.

SPRITE:	A thousand! (aside) There my purse runs out.
PHIDDLE:	All done? Right, going, going, gone!
SPRITE:	(handing PHIDDLE money) One thousand and my hand thereon. (aside) So much for battle number two! (to them, raising hat) Goodday, gents all!
DEMON:	Oh, go and stew!

(SPRITE exits, R., laughing.)

PHADDLE:	Ooh, temper.
PHIDDLE:	Yes, come come, let's go. I fear he's rather crude, you know.

(PHIDDLE and PHADDLE exeunt R. DEMON starts to remove tray.)

DEMON:	Good riddance too. (upsets tray) Oh, blow this tray! It really seems it's not my day.

DEMON: (continued - gathering things onto tray, then
removing disguise and putting that on tray also)
I've other troubles too, alack.
My haughty spell's rebounded back.
Which means that I have got once more
To fix the Princess, what a bore.
And tricky, too. No, wait, I know -
Unto the Ogre she must go.
But who's to take her? Let me see.

(Puts tray and contents off. PHIDDLE and PHADDLE re-enter R.)

PHIDDLE: Come on.

DEMON: (shrugging resignedly)
I s'ppose 'twill have to be.

PHIDDLE: One thousand nicker! Lovely grub,
I bet those rabbits now she'll snub.

DEMON: Alas, alas, she won't indeed.

PHADDLE: Coo, him what taught us how to read.

DEMON: Yes, here to help you once again.
That Princess you will woo in vain.
She's grown so proud of late, dear sir,
There's only one could humble her.
And that's the Ogre Greedyguts.
Take her to him!

PHIDDLE: You must be nuts!
He'd scare us into fifty fits!

PHADDLE: And tear us into little bits!

DEMON: No, no, he would reward ye well.
Besides, I'd hate to have to tell
Just how you gain'd that money there.

PHIDDLE: (clutching it to him)
What's this? Oh, no! You wouldn't dare!

DEMON: Forgery gets a longish time.

PHADDLE: But kidnapping's a naughty crime.

DEMON: I know, but you'll find in a trice
It's naughtiness that makes crime nice!
And I should know, for I'm, I ween,
The oldest crim'nal ever seen.

(Close traverse tabs slowly during number. Fly out cloth.)

MUSIC 30. "YAH! BOO! HISS!"

DEMON: I'm the grand old man of crime
ALL: Yah, boo, hiss!
DEMON: I've done terrible things in my time,
Just like this!

I-4-44

PHIDDLE & PHADDLE:	We are trying to learn the job, To say rude words and to spit and rob And sell you old programmes for Twenty-five bob!
ALL:	Yah, boo, hiss!
ALL:	Three most terrible types are we - Yah! Hiss! Boo! We pour medicine in your tea - And the same to you!
PHIDDLE: PHADDLE: DEMON:	We fill your T.V. with dashes and dots, And mess up your essay with inky blots, And see ev'ry cake gets you covered with spots -
ALL:	Yah! Hiss! Boo! We're a committee of criminal cads - Boo! Hiss! Yah! You will never find lousier lads Than we three are. We're always up to our dirty tricks, Like filling your shoes half full of bricks, And making your lollies fall off their sticks - Boo! Hiss! Yah!

(BLACKOUT.
 Open traverse tabs.)

Scene Five - THE ORANGE GROVE BESIDE THE LAKE

(Fullset. Cut-out ground-row showing lake at back of rostrum, which represents mossy bank. Wings of Orange Trees L. and R. A large dandelion with seed head growing R. on rostrum. Early morning light to open. EFFECTS 20. Alarm clock bell rings, a searching hand appears, finds dandelion and plucks it. Bell stops. SPRITE emerges yawning with dandelion, and is about to blow it when a bird is heard singing off R. EFFECTS 21. She stops and listens and another bird is heard L. EFFECTS 22. She turns towards that, sighs, throws dandelion away and looks sorrowfully over her shoulder at her wingless back. MUSIC 31 - Ballet, in which the SPRITE indicates her yearning for wings and at times pretends she is flying. The Ballet can be built up with the CHORUS entering as birds, insects and bats, who show the SPRITE how they fly and she tries to imitate them. During Ballet LIGHTS COME UP TO FULL. ALL exit at end of Ballet.)

PUSS: (off L.) Come on, Master, this way.

(SPRITE looks off L., pats her back, nods and runs off R., as if she can almost feel her wings sprouting. PUSS and PHILIP enter L.)

And here we are.

PHILIP: Very nice too, but why are we here, Puss?

PUSS: For the picnic, of course. Have you forgotten, Master, it's tomorrow now. And a lovely day tomorrow is, isn't it? Oh, by the way, it's a Royal picnic you know.

PHILIP: Royal picnic?

PUSS: Yes. So in your conversation drop a few casual references to your estates and your castle and so on.

PHILIP: But, Puss, it's so silly. I haven't any estates, or a castle.

PUSS: Ah, but the Marquess of Carabas has. And I'll provide you with them in time, never fear. But now you must go for a bathe in the lake.

PHILIP: A bathe in the lake? Brrr. No thank you.

PUSS: Oh, it's essential, otherwise I'll never get you dressed.

PHILIP: But I should have to get undressed to bathe.

PUSS: Precisely. So be a good master and run along and bathe. (bustling him off and indicating R. wing) And - er - throw your clothes by that tree there.

PHILIP: (laughs) Righto, Puss. (exit R. on rostrum)

PUSS: Poor master. I hope the royal party isn't late. It is a trifle nippy.

(MUSIC 32. NEDDY runs on L.)

NEDDY: Ee-aw!

PUSS: Neddy! Well, well, what a surprise.

(NEDDY gives a hoof to shake.)

I suppose this means Phiddle and Phaddle are near at hand.

(NEDDY nods and whispers in PUSS's ear.)

What, they're going to kidnap the Princess?

(NEDDY nods.)

Hm, good!

(NEDDY looks up surprised.)

It's all right, I mean it will fit in very nicely with my plans.

PHILIP: (off R.) There are my clothes, Puss, take care of them.

(Clothes thrown on by wing R.)

PUSS: (to NEDDY) Ssh! (calling off) Thank you, master. I'll take care of them all right. (picks up clothes) Yes, Neddy, there's a little something you could do for me. Get rid of these clothes.

(NEDDY shows great surprise.)

(draping clothes over him) Well, one always starts a new life without clothes, you know. Just dump them in a ditch or something as far away from here as possible. Thank you, Neddy, bye-bye.

(Exit R. on rostrum. NEDDY, still very surprised, wanders R. shaking head. Sees bell plant, looks around to make sure no one is watching and creeps towards plant. EFFECTS 23. BELLS JINGLE. AUDIENCE shout. NEDDY moves back hastily. JIMOTHY runs on L., carrying a large beach ball.)

JIMOTHY: Coming, thank you. Oh, you naughty donkey.

(NEDDY hangs head in shame.)

Yes, I should just think you are ashamed. Now you go straight home and don't try to pinch anything else.

(NEDDY shakes head, waves a hoof and trots off R.)

I wonder what he's got all those clothes on him for. Perhaps he's a clothes donkey like a clothes horse.

(QUEEN and KING enter L., wearing beach robes. JIMOTHY moves to them.)

QUEEN: Ah, what a superb sylvan setting for our buccolic barbeque, eh, Marmaduke?

KING: Oh yes, very - er - bosky. Shall we take our - er - before we - er - sort of sharpens the - er - doesn't it?

QUEEN: Oh, like anything. Will you join us in the lake, Jimothy?

JIMOTHY: Yes, your Majesty. I never miss my annual dip. I've got my costume on underneath.

I - 5 - 47

(Helps them to remove beach robes revealing Victorian bathing costumes. JIMOTHY gives QUEEN beach ball.)

JIMOTHY: (continued) Excuse me, your Majesties, I'll just find a tree with a peg on it. (exits R.)

QUEEN: (bouncing beach ball to KING) Ah me - this makes me feel quite young.

KING: (bouncing it back) Ah you - you are quite young.

(MUSIC 33. Comic Beach Ball Ballet, in which JIMOTHY joins, also in Victorian bathing costume. At end of dance enter L. PRINCESS, MARY and CHORUS all laughing and chattering. 1st and 2nd CHORUS carry KING and QUEEN's other costumes.)

QUEEN: Ah, Esmerelda, we're just about to take our dip and then I expect the Marquess will be here soon.

PUSS: (off R.) Help! Help! (runs in R. on rostrum) Help for my Master, the Marquess of Carabas!

OTHERS: What's the matter? What's happened? Etc.

PUSS: Oh, your Majesties, my noble master has been set upon and robbed.

OTHERS: Robbed!

PUSS: Yes, and not only was the gift of gold he had brought for your Majesties taken -

KING: Pity.

PUSS: But the wretched thieves stripped every stitch of clothing from his back. My poor master has been forced to hide in the lake.

PRINCESS: How dreadful!

PHILIP: (off R.) Puss, my clothes. Where are my clothes? My shirt -

PUSS: Silk - the very finest silk.

PHILIP: (off) My trunks -

PUSS: Slashed velvet, satin lined.

PHILIP: (off) My jerkin -

PUSS: Cloth of gold, no less.

PHILIP: Where are they all?

PUSS: Alas, Master, I know not.

PRINCESS: Father, we must do something. The poor Marquess will die of cold.

KING: Yes, of course, but what shall we - er - knitting needles?

PRINCESS: No, I have it, father - your clothes; the ones you brought to change into. (takes them from 1st Ch.) Take these to your master.

PUSS: (taking them and bowing to KING) Your Majesty, my master will be deeply grateful.

KING: Yes, I'm sure he - er - that's my best - er -

PHILIP: (off) Puss, my clothes!

PUSS: Yes, master, I have them. (exit R. on rostrum)

QUEEN: Well, how fortunate we were able to help the Marquess.

(Enter ROWLEY L., pushing picnic basket (large skip).)

Ah, food.

ROWLEY: Yes, and I should think we'll all get indigestion. It's jolly heavy food.

QUEEN: Dear, dear, what can Lord Snoozle have put in?

(Lifts lid. SNOOZLE sits up yawning.)

ALL: Snoozle!

SNOOZLE: Well, bless my sandwiches and swiss rolls, where am I?

QUEEN: Tucked in the tuck box. But what have you done with the food?

SNOOZLE: (climbing out) The food? Oh, yes, I was just going to pack it when I must have - er - dropped off and dropped in.

QUEEN: Well, you'd better pop straight back and get it. You go with him, Rowley and get another suit of clothes for the King.

ROWLEY: Righto.

SNOOZLE: Very well, your Majesty. (pushing basket off and yawning) This country air makes me feel quite drowsy.

(They exit L. PUSS enters R. on rostrum.)

PUSS: Your Majesties, my master, the Marquess of Carabas.

(He bows. PHILIP enters R., magnificently dressed. CHORUS bow and curtsey.)

PRINCESS: How handsome!

QUEEN: How noble!

KING: How well dressed!

PUSS: (aside) Bow.

PHILIP: (bows, a little awkwardly) Your Majesties.

QUEEN: Delighted to meet you, Marquess.

PHILIP: Oh - er - yes. (aside) What now?

PUSS: (aside) Bow again.

(PHILIP bows.)

QUEEN: And this is our daughter, Esmerelda.

PHILIP: (staring at her) Yes, I -
PUSS: (nudging him) Bow.

(PHILIP bows.)

QUEEN: What a most unfortunate experience you have had, Marquess.

PHILIP: Oh - er - (aside) Bow?

PUSS: (aside) Don't bow. (to QUEEN) My master is touched by your thought for his welfare, your Majesty, but I fear he is still a little shaken by the incident.

QUEEN: I'm sure he must be. Come, Marmaduke, let us have our bathe and leave the Marquess to recover in peace. It will be an excellent opportunity for him to become acquainted with Esmerelda.

KING: Yes, Queenie. Come, Jim - er - oh, the court may with - er - bye-bye.

(KING, QUEEN, JIMOTHY and 1st and 2nd CHORUS exit R. on rostrum. CHORUS and MARY bow themselves out L. and R. PUSS bows and nudges PHILIP, who does likewise.

PHILIP: (aside) I'm getting giddy with all this bobbing up and down.

PUSS: (aside) You're doing very well, but remember - the estates, the castle. (bows to PRINCESS) Your Highness. (exit R.)

PHILIP: Puss, don't - ! (turns to PRINCESS) I - er, I - er,

PRINCESS: Yes, Marquess?

PHILIP: Oh dear, I do wish I was more used to being a Marquess.

PRINCESS: You mean you've only just come into the title?

PHILIP: Er - you might say that, yes. I'd be much happier if you'd call me Philip.

PRINCESS: Philip? That's funny, I met a Philip the other day, but he was a commoner.

PHILIP: I don't see what's wrong with that.

PRINCESS: No, I'm rather puzzled by it myself. But I don't seem to be able to like commoners any more.

PHILIP: Oh. (to himself) Perhaps Puss is right. (to her) At my - er - my castle I never have any commoners.

PRINCESS: You have a castle?

PHILIP: Oh yes, and estates, and - er - er -

PUSS: (looking on R.) A palace. (withdraws)

PRINCESS: A palace?

PHILIP: Oh - er - yes, a palace. Just a small one, you know. Just the right size for two.

I - 5 - 50

PRINCESS: A palace for two. That sounds nice.

PHILIP: Well, it would be, if I had someone like you to share it.

MUSIC 34. "PALACE FOR TWO"

BOTH:
Let's find a dear little palace,
A huge tiny palace,
And let's live there happy evermore.
With all mod cons and plumbing
And the right tradesmen coming
And the words "No Callers" on the door.

We'll have a garden to sit in,
And I'll/you'll do my/your knittin'
While I/you paint the place to look like new,
We've built in central heating to withstand the wildest weather;
We'll do without one up, one down, and have them both together.
And soon our little nest will have some new wings on view.
In our little palace for two.

(Exeunt R. Enter ROWLEY L. with clothes.)

ROWLEY: Lord Snoozle! Lord Snoozle! Lost him. Oh well, I'd better take these to the King and then try and find him.

(Exit R. MUSIC 35. PHIDDLE looks on L.)

PHIDDLE: (whispering) All clear. Come on, but quietly.

(Creeps on stealthily and suddenly stops R.C. listening. He wears a long black cloak, black floppy-brimmed hat, a black moustache and has a pair of binoculars on a strap round his neck, a pistol in his belt and carries a cosh.)

Hist!

(PHADDLE enters L., similarly disguised but without moustache, and also carrying cosh.)

PHADDLE: What are you doing?

PHIDDLE: (whispering) Ssh! Lower your voice.

PHADDLE: (in very deep voice) What are you doing?

PHIDDLE: I mean, speak quietly. If we're going to kidnap the Princess we must do it unobserved, so I'm listening to make sure there's nobody here.

PHADDLE: And is there?

PHIDDLE: I don't think so, but have a look round with these binoculars. (hands PHADDLE binoculars.)

PHADDLE: Right. (puts them to his eyes and moves away pulling PHIDDLE with him.)

I - 5 - 51

PHIDDLE: Well, let me get the strap off first.

PHADDLE: Oh, sorry.

(PHIDDLE removes strap and takes out pistol to examine while PHADDLE strides round stage looking through binoculars the wrong way round.)

PHIDDLE: See anybody?

PHADDLE: No, no, no. (stopping L.C. and focusing on PHIDDLE's back.) Yes!

PHIDDLE: Who?

PHADDLE: I think he's a midget, but he's got his back to me.

PHIDDLE: Well, creep a bit nearer to him and if he looks suspicious - biff him!

PHADDLE: All right. (creeps up behind PHIDDLE) Oh, he looks very suspicious. He's got a pistol.

PHIDDLE: Then biff him!

(PHADDLE does. PHIDDLE spins round rubbing head.)

OW! What are you playing at?

PHADDLE: Well, you said to -

(PHIDDLE pulls binoculars down from his eyes.)

Hullo, where's the midget gone?

PHIDDLE: There wasn't one. You were looking through the wrong end.

PHADDLE: (puts binoculars to eyes right way) Oh yes. He's a giant. He still looks suspicious though. He's got a great big false moustache. (biffs PHIDDLE)

PHIDDLE: OW! Will you stop knocking me on the nut!

PHADDLE: I'm not, I'm knocking - (lowers binoculars) Oh. Well, you shouldn't go around disguised as a giant midget.

PHIDDLE: But I - oh, never mind. Did you make those masks like I told you?

PHADDLE: (producing two black masks) Yes, here they are.

QUEEN: (off R.) Esmerelda, see if Lord Snoozle's arrived with the food yet.

PRINCESS: (off R.) All right, mother.

PHIDDLE: The Princess! Quick, put 'em on and hide behind that tree.

(They put the masks on.)

PHADDLE: Ooh, it's gone all dark.

PHIDDLE: (pushing mask away from eyes) You haven't put any eye holes in them!

(Bundles PHADDLE off above wing L. PRINCESS enters R.)

PRINCESS: No sign of Snoozle here. Perhaps he's coming along the road. (moves to look off below wing L.)

(PHIDDLE and PHADDLE peer on at her above wing. PUSS creeps on R. on rostrum. Exit PRINCESS below wing with PHIDDLE and PHADDLE creeping after her. PUSS jumps down from rostrum.)

PUSS: Time for a little intervention, I think. (softly calling) Master. (exits R.)

(PRINCESS enters L. above wing, PHIDDLE and PHADDLE still creeping behind her.)

PRINCESS: I wonder where he's got to. There's not a soul in sight.

(PHIDDLE and PHADDLE grab PRINCESS, PHIDDLE putting a hand over her mouth. PHILIP enters R., looking back.)

PHILIP: Yes, Puss, what is -
PHIDDLE: (taking hand from her mouth) OW! She bit!) (together)
PRINCESS: Help! Help!)

(PHILIP spins round.)

PHILIP: Esmerelda!)
PHIDDLE &) (together)
PHADDLE: Philip!)

(They pull their hats down over their faces as PHILIP rushes at them.)

PHILIP: You villains! Take that! And that!

(Shouts and cries from them as he knocks them away and they stumble off L. Enter PUSS R.)

PUSS: Bravo, master! (calling off R.) Your Majesties! Everybody! Come quickly! Come quickly!

PHILIP: Esmerelda, are you all right?

(KING, QUEEN, JIMOTHY, all fully dressed again, and ROWLEY, MARY and CHORUS all hurry on R.)

ALL: What's happened? What's the commotion? Etc.

PUSS: Your Majesties, the Marquess has just saved your daughter's life!

(Exclamations from everybody.)

I fear it must have been those thieves again, but my master bravely beat them off.

(Exclamations of approbation.)

QUEEN: Oh, Marmaduke, how can we ever repay him?
KING: I think the usual - er - highly suitable.
QUEEN: Her hand in marriage? Excellent!

PHILIP:	Your Majesties!)	(together)
PRINCESS:	Mother!)	
PUSS:	(aside) See, master?	

QUEEN: And we'll have a grand ball forthwith to celebrate the betrothal.

ALL: Hurrah!

MUSIC 36. "ANTHEM" (Reprise)

QUEEN: For this great occasion
　　　　Let festivities commence.
　　　　We ordain a wondrous ball.

KING: Admission eighteen pence.

PUSS: Come salute our hero,
　　　　And his future let all bless.

PHILIP: I have done so little though,
　　　　To win this sweet Princess.

ALL: For this handsome man and maid
　　　Much glory we foretell.
　　　Hurry to the Palace:
　　　Decorate the Palace:
　　　You'll dance at the Palace,
　　　And we'll be there as well.

(Triumphant march round.

CURTAIN.

CURTAIN UP for picture with DEMON U.L. shaking fist and SPRITE U.R. poking long nose at him.

CURTAIN.)

(MUSIC 37. Entr'acte.)

PART TWO

Scene Six - THE BALLROOM AT THE PALACE

(Fullset. Ballroom cut-out ground-row at back of rostrum. Double thrones in C. of rostrum and steps down in front. Wings L. and R. (Scene Three set could be used again without the dais.) CHORUS, as courtiers, and ROWLEY discovered. MUSIC 38. Fanfare sounds as Curtain rises and opening music starts. JIMOTHY enters L.)

JIMOTHY: Make way, make way -
Here come their Royal Majesties,
Make way.

(Bows. CHORUS bow and curtsey to KING and QUEEN as they enter very grandly L. KING trips as he enters.)

QUEEN: Marmaduke!

KING: Sorry, my - er - slight slip of the - er -

(QUEEN falls up steps.)

See what I mean.

(They take their places on throne. MARY enters R.)

MARY: Make way, make way -
Here comes her Royal Highness too,
Make way.

(She curtsies. CHORUS bow and curtsey to PRINCESS as she enters R. She moves to foot of steps R.C. and curtsies to KING and QUEEN. PUSS enters L.)

PUSS: Make way, make way -
Here comes the Royal groom to be,
Make way.

(He bows. CHORUS bow and curtsey to PHILIP as he enters L. and moves to foot of steps L.C. and bows to KING and QUEEN. KING rises, bows and proffers hand to QUEEN, who graciously inclines her head, rises and takes hand and they move down steps. ALL bow and curtsey as they pass. PHILIP offers his arm to ESMERELDA, JIMOTHY to MARY, PUSS and ROWLEY each to a CHORUS girl and CHORUS boys to girls.)

MUSIC 38. "TWISTED GAVOTTE"

ALL: Such an introduction signified
We should dance a measure dignified.
Lords and Ladies, hand in hand,
Try to keep rhythm with the band.
Forward, turn and then reversal
With a mere three weeks rehearsal.
What more modern dance has got
The charm of the Gavotte?

JIMOTHY & MARY:	It's very nice, but we declare It seems to us a little square.
PHILIP & PRINCESS:	Yes, we agree, so let's advance And try out a modern dance.
(Viennese Waltz.)	
JIMOTHY & MARY:	We fear that we will carping sound, But this one seems a little round.
KING & QUEEN:	Yes, we agree, etc.
(Polka.)	
JIMOTHY & MARY:	Though you may think we are wrong, We feel that this is oblong.
PUSS & CH GIRL:	Yes, we agree, etc.
(Rumba.)	
JIMOTHY & MARY:	To give offence we'd avoid, But Rumba is rather rhomboid!
ROWLEY & CH GIRL:	Yes, we agree, etc.
(Charleston.)	
JIMOTHY & MARY:	The years roll by, it ain't fair, Ev'ry old dance is so square. You will agree when we advance To a really modern dance.

(Finale of whatever is the current dance rage, ending with collapse of KING and QUEEN in C. and exit of everybody else.)

QUEEN: Ooh! I think I'd better sit the next fifteen dances out. (endeavours to rise) Right here.

KING: Oh, come, come, Queenie, there's nothing to - er - (rising with some difficulty) Ooh! Ow! Ouch! See? Excruciatingly painless.

QUEEN: (rising) Well, I'll take your wooooor! Oh, Marmaduke, you fibber! Well, now I must see that all the arrangements are complete for our little choral offering later. Ring for Lord Snoozle, dear.

KING: (looking round R. for a bell) Yes, my - er - there doesn't seem to - er - oh, I'll take one of these and - er -

(Puts hand to bell plant. EFFECTS 24. BELLS JINGLE   AUDIENCE shout. JIMOTHY and MARY run on R., backwards.)

JIMOTHY: Thank you. Oh. You - er - rang, your Majesty?

KING: No, not exac - er - her Majesty wants Lord - er - where is he?

JIMOTHY: Lord Snoozle? Nobody knows. He hasn't been seen since he came back for the picnic basket yesterday.

II - 6 - 56

MARY: Perhaps he's gone into hibernation.

QUEEN: I hope not. I wanted to ask him if the musicians I ordered had turned up. Have you seen any musicians walking around?

MARY: Not walking around, but there are some captive ones down there. (points to ORCHESTRA)

QUEEN: Oh yes, I know those, but it's Signor Umpah and his Orchestra I'm looking for at the moment. See if you can find them, dears. And send them to me in the Salon.

MARY &
JIMOTHY: Yes, your Majesty. (They exit R.)

KING: But we haven't got a - have we?

QUEEN: No, I know, but it sounds good.

(They exit L. Enter PHILIP and PRINCESS R.)

PHILIP: I wonder where everybody's disappeared?

PRINCESS: Maybe father ordered free refreshments. I think I should tell you, we're really very poor, you know.

PHILIP: And I think I should tell you, I'm really -

(Enter PUSS L., he bows to them and exits D.L.)

PRINCESS: Yes, you're really?

PHILIP: I'm really very much in love with you. So whether you're poor or I'm - well, after all, nobody's quite what they seem.

MUSIC 39. "WHOEVER YOU ARE"

(They exit R. BLUE SPOT UP L. DEMON looks on.)

DEMON: I'll cross my fingers, cross my toes,
And p'raps this time - one never knows. (leaps on)
No, not a sausage, how unfair.

(BLUE FLASH U.L. on rostrum, startling him.)

Aha! What's it doing right up there?
I have brought hence that doltish twain
To try their kidnap bid again.
But this time, just to lull suspicions,
I have disguis'd them as musicians.
(calling off L.)
Come, Phiddle! Phaddle! Come, you two! (pause)
Not there? Well where? P'rhaps in the -

(PHIDDLE and PHADDLE look on R.)

PHIDDLE & PHADDLE: Boo!

(DEMON is surprised. They enter R., dressed in Victorian evening dress. Each carries a music stand, some music and a large instrument case. PHADDLE also carries a small gilt chair, which he places R.C.)

DEMON:		You naughty lads, don't muck about, Or I'll be forc'd your lugs to clout. Now list, this time I want success, So ere you kidnap the Princess, First grab the cat and steal his boots. Got that?
PHIDDLE:		(taking out little book and making note) Yes, yes, steal daisy roots.
DEMON:		Next, bring the Princess where I wait. Got that as well?
PHIDDLE:		(making note) Yes, all down, mate.
DEMON:		Then one of you must come right back To put young Philip on the rack. Say 'twas his doing and what's more -
PHIDDLE:		That he's a whatsit - Impost<u>o</u>r!
DEMON:		Quite right, good lad. Meanwhile will I With Princess to the Ogre fly, Whence later you can follow me That you may well rewarded be. All happy?
PHIDDLE:		Yes.
PHADDLE:		Well, I'm not struck.
DEMON:		Think of the lolly! Well, good luck!

(Exit L. BLUE SPOT OUT.)

PHADDLE: Lolly! I'm doing this for my guppies, not lolly. They don't like lollies anyway.

PHIDDLE: Oh, belt up about your guppies. There's someone coming. Look like a musician.

(Each takes out a rather full, curly-haired wig and puts it on. Enter QUEEN L.)

QUEEN:	Ah, Signor Umpah.
PHIDDLE:	Have you? I didn't know I'd got it on.
QUEEN:	Aren't you Signor Umpah, the musician?
PHIDDLE:	What? Oh. (very Italian, suddenly) Oh, yesa. So sorry, my Marmaladia is not so hots. I am Signor Umpah, yesa.
QUEEN:	Splendid. And where is your Orchestra?
PHIDDLE:	(points to PHADDLE) Here.
QUEEN:	Hm, rather small.
PHIDDLE:	Yesa, but he's nota finished growing yeta.
QUEEN:	Perhaps you play as well?

PHIDDLE: Me, I playa the wiggle-waggle.

QUEEN: The wiggle-waggle? What's that?

PHIDDLE: Thisa. (opens instrument case and takes out conductor's baton)

QUEEN: What does he play?

(PHADDLE opens his case and takes out a small triangle.)

PHIDDLE: Thata.

QUEEN: But surely you can't play much with that?

PHIDDLE: Oh, yesa. We playa the Triangle Concerto for you, ha? (raises baton then lowers it) No, waita. We can't playa the Triangle Concerto in a ballroom.

QUEEN: Why not?

PHIDDLE: 'Cos itsa Triangle Concerto in A flat. I know, we playa the Triangle Voluntary.

(PHADDLE sits on chair and arranges music. PHIDDLE taps stand and raises baton, and gives downbeat to PHADDLE, who plays one 'ting'.

You likea?

QUEEN: Haven't you a slightly longer piece?

PHIDDLE: Yesa. As you makea the request we playa the "Bus Conductor's Rhapsody".

(Taps music stand again, raises baton and gives downbeat. PHADDLE plays two sharp tings.)

QUEEN: Does it stop there?

PHIDDLE: No, with two tings it starta.

QUEEN: What happens then?

PHIDDLE: We reacha the terminus.

(Enter KING, MARY, JIMOTHY, ROWLEY and CHORUS L., with music sheets.)

QUEEN: Ah, here's our little choral group. You know, Signor Umpah, I think it might be better if your - er - orchestra joined in the singing rather than playing.

PHIDDLE: All righta. He singa and I conductor you all, ha? Whatsa the song?

JIMOTHY: (handing some music sheets to QUEEN) Well, a bloke called Mozart and me have just written a song all about Mary, your Majesty.

QUEEN: Ah, delightful. (handing music sheet to PHIDDLE) Here you are then, Signor Umpah, a little piece entitled "Mistress Mary Quite Contrary".

II - 6 - 59

PHIDDLE: Yes, she'sa a very nicea little piece too. (raising baton) Er-onea, er-twoa, er-threea -

MUSIC 40. "MISTRESS MARY QUITE CONTRARY" (based on an aria by Mozart.)

ALL:
Mistress Mary Quite Contrary,
Mistress Mary Quite Contrary,
How does your garden grow?
How does your garden grow?
Mistress Mary Quite Contrary,
How does your garden grow?
Silver bells and cockle shells,
Silver bells and cockle shells,
Silver bells and cockle shells.
Pretty maids,
Pretty maids all in a row.
Pretty maids,
Pretty maids all in a row.
Mistress Mary Quite Contrary,
Mistress Mary Quite Contrary,
How does your garden grow?
How does your garden grow?
How does your garden grow?
How does your garden grow?
With silver bells and cockle shells,
Pretty maids all in a row,
Pretty maids all in a row.
With silver bells
With bells,
With bells,
And pretty maids all in a row.
With silver bells and cockle shells,
And pretty maids all in a row,
Pretty maids all in a row.
O Mistress, Mistress Mary,
O Mary Quite Contrary,
How does your garden grow?
- den grow?
How does your garden grow?

(They bow to their applause. EFFECT 25. Gong sounds off R.)

QUEEN: Tea's up!

(ALL run off R. Enter PUSS L.)

PUSS: Bless my paws and whiskers, where's everybody running to? They must have been frightened by those curious noises I heard just now. Give me caterwuling any time.

(PHIDDLE and PHADDLE look on R. on rostrum.)

Hm, I wonder what it's like to be a King? (sits on throne)

(PHIDDLE and PHADDLE nod to each other and creep behind thrones.)

PUSS: (continued) Not very impressive. I think I prefer being a cat.

(PHIDDLE and PHADDLE appear on either side of thrones.)

Especially now I'm a talking cat.

(PHIDDLE and PHADDLE grab a boot each and start to tug them off PUSS's feet. BLACKOUT. WHITE FLASH. Exit talking PUSS. Enter MIME PUSS. LIGHTS UP. MIME PUSS is mewing loudly and trying to get boots from PHIDDLE and PHADDLE.)

PHIDDLE: Success!

PRINCESS: (off L.) Puss, is that you, Puss?

PHIDDLE: The Princess! (takes out chloroform bottle and a pad. Soaking pad) We'll be a bit more subtle this time. Here, hold this. (gives pad to PHADDLE and replaces bottle)

PHADDLE: What is it?

PHIDDLE: Chloroform.

PHADDLE: (sniffing it appreciatively) Oh yes. Smells nice.

PHIDDLE: (snatching it from him) Look out! You'll put yourself out!

(Hides pad behind back as PRINCESS enters L.)

PRINCESS: What's the matter, Puss? Oh, good evening.

PHIDDLE: Good eveninga, your highness.

(PUSS frantically tries to drag her away, they move behind her.)

PRINCESS: What are you in such a state about?

(PHIDDLE clamps pad over her mouth.)

PHIDDLE: There, it's working, it's working -

(She collapses on top of him.)

PHADDLE: It's worked.

PHIDDLE: Well, don't just stand there - get her off me!

(PHADDLE raises her so that PHIDDLE can rise.)

That's it. Now off with her to the Demon!

(They pick her up and carry her off L. PUSS runs to and fro mewing loudly. MUSIC 41. HOUSELIGHTS UP. SPRITE appears at back of auditorium and hurries down to catwalk and onto stage.)

SPRITE: Fiddlededee and fiddlesticks!
Foil'd by Phiddle and Phaddle's tricks.

(MIME PUSS mews imploringly and points L.)

I know, Puss, there's no time to waste,
To get your boots back first I'll haste,
For you're the one must win the day.

II - 6 - 61

(Reaches stage and starts to go R. PUSS stops her and points L. House lights out.)

SPRITE: (continued) No, out the back's the quickest way.

(Runs off R. KING, QUEEN and PHILIP enter L. ROWLEY enters R., CHORUS L. and R. KING and QUEEN move to throne.)

QUEEN: Well, Marmaduke, I think it's time we made the official announcement of the betrothal.

KING: Yes, but where's - er - I think she should be - er - don't you?

QUEEN: You're perfectly right, Marmaduke.

(Enter MARY and JIMOTHY R.)

Jimothy, ask her Highness to join us.

JIMOTHY: We've just been looking for her, your Majesty.

MARY: But she's nowhere to be found.

(Enter PHIDDLE L., without wig and with cloak covering musicians costume.)

PHIDDLE: Your Majesties, that man has had your daughter stolen away. (points at PHILIP)

PHILIP: What! But that's ridiculous!   )

OTHERS: The Princess! Stolen away! By the Marquess!)(together)
The Marquess! Etc.   )

PHIDDLE: He's no Marquess. He's the old Miller's son, Philip!

QUEEN: What? An impostor?

PHIDDLE: Yes, I saw him plotting the whole thing with that cat of his.

QUEEN: Seize them! Seize them!

(2 CHORUS men seize PHILIP. ROWLEY moves to take PUSS, who shoots between his legs, knocks him over and runs off R.)

You monster! What have you done with our daughter?

PHILIP: Nothing! I swear I had nothing to do with her disappearance.

QUEEN: Nonsense! Jimothy, put him under guard at the royal barracks.

(PHILIP is dragged off L., with JIMOTHY following.)

The rest of you, search the land from end to end! Our daughter must be found!

MUSIC 42. "FIND HER!"

QUEEN &
OTHERS: My/Her child! My/Her child! Where can she be?
What ending has this tragedy?

QUEEN:	You silly lot of idiots Just echoing what I say, Go and find her!
OTHERS:	We shall find her! We shall find her! We'll find her!

(BLACKOUT.

Close traverse tabs. Fly in frontcloth.)

Scene Seven - OUTSIDE THE PALACE

(Tabs or frontcloth (could use Scene Four cloth). If cloth is used open tabs during scene when ready. BLUE SPOT UP L. DEMON jumps on into it.)

DEMON: Aha? No, foil'd again, I see.
Oh, I could spit.

(Does so. FLASH L., to his great surprise.)

Bad gracious me!
Well, things are looking up all round,
I have achieved in but one bound -
One speechless cat, one lad in clink,
One filch'd Princess - not bad, I think.
Ah, here she's brought.

PHADDLE: (entering R.) Ow! Leggo, miss!

(He is followed by PRINCESS, holding one arm in a half-nelson. In his free hand he carries PUSS's boots.

Hey! Help! She's hurting!

DEMON: What means this?

PHADDLE: She pounc'd and took me by surprise
When Phiddle went to tell his lies.

DEMON: Hush, hush! Be quiet, you silly dunce!
Princess, unhand that man at once!

PRINCESS: No fear! To kidnap me he tried.

DEMON: On orders that I had supplied.

PRINCESS: Then I shall twist your arm as well.

(Grabs DEMON's arm and holds it in half-nelson.)

DEMON: Ow! What's my petrifying spell?
With marble flesh and ramrod bone,
Be for awhile turn'd into stone.

(Music ting. PRINCESS drops their arms and stands rigid.)

Thank badness! I'll with her away
Ere she's restor'd. Come.

(Moves L. a step. She does not move. Tugs at her.)

Come, I say!
Oh, Oldbad, use your brain, not force.
Be turn'd to stepping stone, of course,
And to the Ogre let us go.

(PRINCESS starts to goose-step like an automaton kicking DEMON in behind as she does so.)

Ow! Ouch! Mind where you're stepping though!

(They exit L. MUSIC 43. SPRITE looks on R., as they go and then creeps behind PHADDLE.)

PHADDLE: Ooh, my arm, it's broke for sure.
I'll not go kidnapping no more.

(Music ting as SPRITE taps him on head with wand and points to boots.)

I've had a thought, this kind of boot
My dainty plates would nicely suit.

(SPRITE nods and touches boots with wand, 2 music tings, then PHADDLE starts to put boots on, leaving his own in C.)

SPRITE: (aside) If my spell works, then soon will he
Much rather of those boots be free.
So I'll fetch Puss his chance to wait
While Phiddle learns his brother's fate. (exit R.)

PHIDDLE: (off R.) Hey, Phaddle!

(Enters R., just as PHADDLE finishes putting boots on.)

Phaddle.

(Music ting.)

PHADDLE: (getting onto all fours) Miaow!

PHIDDLE: Eh?

PHADDLE: Miaow!

PHIDDLE: What do you think you're doing? You'll get all mucky playing about on the ground like that.

PHADDLE: (nods, sits on his haunches and starts to wash himself like a cat) Miaow.

PHIDDLE: And why do you keep saying "Miaow"? You're not a cat.

PHADDLE: (nods) Miaow. (purrs and rubs his head against PHIDDLE's legs.)

(2 CHORUS enter L.)

PHIDDLE: Here, nark it! Nark it!

(But PHADDLE continues. The CHORUS stop and stare and PHIDDLE tries to pretend nothing is happening. The CHORUS giggle, turn and run off L.)

You'll have people thinking we're bonkers. (sees PHADDLE's boots) And what have you taken your boots off for? Oh, I see, you've put the cat's boots on - wait a minute, that's it, that's what's turned you into a cat. Here, get 'em off, get 'em -

(The first 2 CHORUS enter with another pair and point to PHIDDLE and PHADDLE and giggle.)

Oh dear. (to them) Er - he's lost something. Yes. I'm just going to give him a hand to look for it.

(Gets on all fours and pretends to search. PHADDLE regards him quizzically for a moment, then puts out a playful paw to PHIDDLE's face. CHORUS laugh.)

PHIDDLE: (continued) Er - yes. I think you're right, more over this way.

(Turns to search R. as two other CHORUS enter R. and stare at him. The others whisper and giggle, then decide to try something and one throws a piece of screwed-up paper tied to a piece of string. PHADDLE leaps towards it. The CHORUS GIRL pulls it away, then throws it back and starts to pull it slowly along the ground, while PHADDLE stalks it cat-like. PHIDDLE turns and sees what is going on.)

Hey, no, don't tease him like that. He can't help thinking he's a cat at the moment. He - (a brilliant idea strikes him) As a matter of fact, he is a cat, and I'm a dog - a mad one!

(Growls and barks fiercely then rushes towards the CHORUS L., they scream and run off; he turns and does the same, with the same effect, to the CHORUS R. Is amazed by this, and now arches his back and hisses and spits at PHIDDLE, then leaps furiously at him trying to claw him with his hands.)

Ouch! No! Stop it! I'm not really a dog! Stop! (manages to rise) There, there, good Puss. But let me just take those boots off.

(There is another struggle, but PHIDDLE manages to get PHADDLE onto his back and pulls the boots off with a tug (music ting), falling backwards as he does so. During this the SPRITE looks on R., and beckons off to the MIME PUSS, who also looks on R.)

PHADDLE: (sitting up) Hullo. Here, what have you taken my boots off for?

PHIDDLE: 'Cos they're not safe.

(Throws them behind him to R. SPRITE motions to PUSS to get them but to be quiet. PUSS nods, SPRITE goes and PUSS starts to creep towards boots.)

We'll bury 'em somewhere, but don't you ever put them on any more.

PHADDLE: But they suited me. Hey, look! The cat's got 'em again!

(PUSS scampers off R. with boots as they jump up.)

PHIDDLE: What? Quick! After him! We'll catch him!

(They run off R. Talking PUSS enters L.)

PUSS: I don't think you will, you know. Dear, dear. Phaddle's left his own boots behind.

(PHIDDLE and PHADDLE re-enter running backwards.)

PHADDLE: Well, I can't go running about without anything on my feet. (looks for boots where he left them)

PHIDDLE: (double marking time) Oh, hurry up, then.

PUSS:	Looking for something?
PHADDLE:	Yes, my boots.
PUSS:	Ah, these perhaps?
PHADDLE:	That's right, thanks. (starts to put them on)
PUSS:	Not at all, delighted to oblige. (bows ironically and exits L.)

(Close traverse tabs. Fly out cloth.)

PHADDLE: Right, ready.

(They run R.)

Very polite cat that.

PHIDDLE: Yes, very.

BOTH: Eh?

(They turn and run L. MUSIC 44.)

Hey! You, stop! Wait! Come back!

(BLACKOUT.

Open traverse tabs.)

Scene Eight - THE ROYAL BARRACKS

(Full set. Cut-out ground-row as cell backing set on back of rostrum. Small cell in C. of rostrum composed of bars. The bars can be made in two "L" shaped cut-outs. One arm of each "L" running from the back to the front of the rostrum and the other arms going at right angles along the front of the rostrum, where they are joined together by a barred doorway with a heavy looking lock. Steps down in front of door. Wings L. and R., which should give the set a rather seedy martial air. A bugle hangs on R. wing. D.L. a prop cannon with slender detachable barrel and a pile of rubber and cotton-wool cannon balls beside it; also a rack with a rifle, a halberd and a sword in scabbard with belt. Above weapons 2 bearskin helmets. PHILIP discovered in cell, with JIMOTHY, in a bearskin helmet, marching to and fro. He carries a blunderbuss and has a large bunch of keys at his waist.)

PHILIP: Let me out! Let me out! Jimothy, I've got to find the Princess, please let me out.

JIMOTHY: I wish I could, then I wouldn't have to stay here guarding you. I want to see Mary again. (sighs)

PHILIP: And I want to see Esmerelda. (sighs)

JIMOTHY: It's rotten being in love, isn't it? (sighs)

PHILIP: Yes, marvellous. (sighs)

JIMOTHY: But it's sort of nice at the same time. (sighs)

PHILIP: Um - horrid. (sighs)

MUSIC 45. "BLUNDERFUL LOVE"

BOTH:
Love! Love! Let's not pretend
Love's a mess from beginning to end.
All the opposites under the sun,
It's awfully confusing but ever such fun.

Love's a terrible pain that's so nice.
Love's so hot that it turns you to ice.
Love's an angel when love is a knave.
You're the master when you are the slave.

Love is knowledge when love's a surprise,
Love's most blind when it opens its eyes
You can best see the way the world goes
When love tumbles you flat on your nose!

Love! Love! etc.

(PUSS runs on L.)

PUSS: Master! Master!

JIMOTHY: (bringing blunderbuss down in challenging position, but the wrong way round) Halt! Who goes...ooh, that's wrong. Well, I know who you are, anyway.

PHILIP: Puss! Thank goodness you're here! What's been happening?

PUSS:	Quite a lot. For one thing the Princess is in the hands of the Ogre.
PHILIP & JIM:	What! The Ogre!
PUSS:	Yes. I must say it fits in splendidly with my plans.
PHILIP:	Puss, how can you? We must rescue her at once.
PUSS:	Exactly. It gives us an excellent opportunity to deal with the Ogre. As the Marquess of Carabas you'd have to do that sooner or later.
JIMOTHY:	But he's not the Marquess of Carabas.
PUSS:	No? Well, we'll see when we've rescued the Princess, and to do that you must release my master immediately.
JIMOTHY:	Ooh, I can't do that.
PUSS:	Oh. Are you sure?
JIMOTHY:	Quite sure.
PUSS:	Pity. (moving to look at weapons D.L.) I hate using these kind of methods. Please accept my apologies in advance. Which would you prefer, the cannon barrel or the rifle butt?
JIMOTHY:	Prefer? What for?
PUSS:	To be knocked out with, of course.
JIMOTHY:	Eh?
PHILIP:	Puss, no! You mustn't hurt Jimothy.
PUSS:	Oh no, just a light tap. I think the rifle butt. (taking rifle and swinging it up) Ready?
PHILIP:	Puss, careful! (in his agitation, pushes open cell door) Oh.
PUSS:	(lowers rifle) Ah, splendid. (replaces it) That saves all this nasty force.
JIMOTHY:	Eh? What? Here, how did you get out?

(While his head is turned PUSS takes the key ring from his belt.)

PUSS:	Ah, I'm afraid that was your fault, Jimothy. (gently persuading him into cell and winking at PHILIP.) You see, when you have a prisoner in a cell you must not only - (nods to PHILIP)
PHILIP:	Shut the door - (does so)
PUSS:	But lock it. (does so) Come, master.
JIMOTHY:	I see. Hey, you've locked me in!
PUSS:	(putting keys on rack) That's right. Ah, you'd better take this, master.

(Gives PHILIP the sword, which he buckles on.)

PHILIP:	Thanks, Puss.

PUSS: Come then, master, on to the Ogre!

(They exit L.)

JIMOTHY: But - but...come back! Dirty rotters. I may be stuck here for days. Nobody ever visits the Barracks.

QUEEN: (off R.) This way, Marmaduke.

JIMOTHY: Oh, crikey!

(QUEEN enters R. in the uniform of W.R.A.C. officer. KING follows in battledress and a field marshall's plumed hat with his crown on top of it.)

QUEEN: High time we inspected the army, Marmaduke.

KING: I never knew we had an - er - have we?

QUEEN: Well, there's Jimothy. Oh, Jimothy, dear, there you are. But you should be out here, it's your prisoner who should be in there. And where is your prisoner?

JIMOTHY: (in small voice) Escaped.

KING & QUEEN: Escaped!

QUEEN: But how?

JIMOTHY: I'm not sure. His cat arrived and sort of talked it into happening. And he said the Ogre had got the Princess and they were going to rescue her.

QUEEN: Poppycock!

(MARY runs in backwards with small piece of material.)

MARY: Your Majesties, this piece of the Princess's dress has been found on a thornbush near the Ogre's castle!

OTHERS: What!

KING: Not poppy - er - whatsit.

QUEEN: No, the cat was right, splendid animal. We must go to their aid immediately and besiege the Ogre's castle. Marmaduke, release Jimothy.

(KING picks up key and does so.)

Mary, sound the call for Volunteers!

MARY: Yes, your Majesty. (takes bugle from wall and is about to blow it in QUEEN's ear.)

QUEEN: Not right in the royal lughole, though.

(MARY turns bugle away and blows a blast. NEDDY immediately runs on L., followed by PHIDDLE and PHADDLE.)

PHIDDLE: (as they enter) Hey, Neddy, come back!

NEDDY: Ee-aw!

II - 8 - 70

JIMOTHY: Blimey, that was quick.

QUEEN: Yes indeed. I'm delighted to see you're so keen to fight the Ogre and rescue the Princess.

PHIDDLE: What? Oh - er - yes. Yes.

PHADDLE: I thought you said we were going to the Ogre's to -

PHIDDLE: (clapping hand over his mouth) That's right, going to the Ogre's to fight. (aside to him) Shurrup, we'll have to pretend we're volunteers and slip away when we get the chance.

QUEEN: Excellent recruiting work, Neddy. We'll make you a cavalry regiment for that, if you like.

(NEDDY nods enthusiastically.)

Good. Cavalry regiment - right turn!

(NEDDY front and rear turn R. so that he is facing sideways.)

QUEEN: Quick march!

(NEDDY marches sideways.)

KING: That's not quite - er - is it?

QUEEN: No. Cavalry regiment - halt! Left turn!

(NEDDY halts and turns L., to resume ordinary shape.)

Perhaps he'd do better with a rider. Mary, you're appointed C. in C., Cavalry. Take your regiment on a few manoeuvres while I get the infantry into shape.

MARY: Yes, ma'am. (salutes with R. hand to L. side of head, then tries to mount NEDDY) He's rather high for mounting.

JIMOTHY: I'll crank him down a bit.

(Grasps NEDDY's tail and cranks it up and down. NEDDY sinks down assisted by cranking noises on a ratchet-rattle from ORCHESTRA. MARY mounts the wrong way round. NEDDY straightens up.)

MARY: Gee down, Neddy.

(NEDDY looks round at her, rather puzzled, shakes head in bewilderment and trots off R.)

QUEEN: Now you men are the infantry. Now first you two must be properly dressed, so you'll need bearskins.

PHIDDLE: But then we'll be properly undressed.

PHADDLE: Here, I'm not going to fight without anything on, I might catch my death.

QUEEN: No, no, I mean these things. These are bearskins. (gives them to PHIDDLE and PHADDLE.)

PHIDDLE &
PHADDLE: Oh. (They put them on.)

QUEEN: Now you must all equip yourselves with arms.

PHADDLE: I brought my own with me. (flaps arms)

JIMOTHY: (beside weapons) These kind of arms.

PHADDLE: Oh.

PHIDDLE: Bags the rifle. (takes it)

KING: Bags the - er - yes. (takes halberd)

PHADDLE: Bags the - (sees only cannon is left) Oh. Oh well. (picks up barrel and a cannon ball) Are these supposed to go with it?

JIMOTHY: Yes.

PHADDLE: (drops it, it bounces) Ooh, look.

QUEEN: Yes, they're very economical. You hit the enemy and then they bounce back.

PHADDLE: But how do you use them with this? Oh, I know. Like this, eh? (bounces cannon ball then hits it off using barrel as a bat) Ooh, this is nice.

(Hits a couple more offstage then, with PHIDDLE's assistance, knocks some of the cotton wool into AUDIENCE.)

QUEEN: Cease fire! That's enough artillery practice, you're wasting ammunition. Besides, they're friends. (to AUDIENCE) I do hope you understand, just a little natural exuberance. Now we're ready to fall in. Marmaduke, you be marker.

(KING takes up a position L.C.)

And the rest of you fall in on him.

(OTHERS look at each other then fall on KING.)

Ah, not quite right. I mean fall in in a line beside him.

OTHERS: Ah.

(They rise and KING resumes position.)

QUEEN: Now - fall in!

(They fall in a line beside KING.)

I don't think you quite understand. To fall in is to stand.

OTHERS: Oh.

(They get in line beside KING, JIMOTHY on his R., then PHIDDLE, then PHADDLE.)

QUEEN: That's it. Now we'll present arms. Do you know how to present arms?

OTHERS: Yes! (They throw the weapons at QUEEN's feet.)

QUEEN: I was afraid that would happen. Pick them up again.

(They do so.)

QUEEN: (continued) This time you must present arms properly.

(They look at each other and move to QUEEN and, politely bowing, place them in her hands then return into line.)

I had a shrewd suspicion that was coming next, too. (throws weapons upstage) We'll try a little marching instead. Army, left turn!

(They turn R.)

As you were.

(They turn back.)

No, that was right so it wasn't right, not for turning left. When you turn left, left's right, but right's not right. After all, there's only one left and one right so if right's not right, what's left? Left - and that's right, right?

OTHERS: Right.

QUEEN: Right. Left turn!

(KING turns L., JIMOTHY turns L. about, PHIDDLE double L. about to end up facing where he started, PHADDLE turns R.)

Still a slight confusion, I see. Perhaps it would speed things up if you just all turned thataway. (points L.)

(KING does double L. about turn, JIMOTHY a one and a half L. about, PHIDDLE a one and a half R. about and PHADDLE a L. about turn.)

That's it. Now you're ready for marching. Quick march!

(KING and PHIDDLE start off with their L. feet, JIMOTHY and PHADDLE with R. feet, so that the 3 behind the KING keep trying to get in step with the one in front.)

Left right, left right. Left wheel!

(They wheel round.)

A little quicker, left right, left right, etc.

(The marching gets quicker and quicker and they bunch up on themselves heading straight for QUEEN.)

Not too quick. Halt! Halt! HALT!

(But they keep moving until she is pressed up against R. wing.)

About turn then! Left turn! Right turn! Fall out!

(They turn and march straight towards AUDIENCE.)

Oh dear! Stop! STOP!

(They stop, poised on the brink.)

Don't go marching over our friends, dears.

(They move back and QUEEN moves to C.

KING: I don't think we're very - er - are we?

QUEEN: Well, I think you might win the No-bull prize. But perhaps

II - 8 - 73

QUEEN: (continued) we're not really cut out for soldiering.

MUSIC 46. "HURRAH FOR THE MILITARY"

ALL: When I went into the Army, boys, I wished I'd gone to sea,
'Cos the only thing that I wanted out of the Army, boys, was me!

JIMOTHY: They got me on to the Barrack's Square
And marching I would be.
Left, right, about turn!

ALL: Hurrah for the Milit'ry!

KING, QUEEN, PHIDDLE & PHADDLE: When I went into the Army, etc.

KING: They got me in the Orderly Room,
And cleaning I would be.
Spit - polish, spit - polish.

JIMOTHY: Left, right, etc.

ALL: Hurrah for the Milit'ry!

QUEEN, PHIDDLE & PHADDLE: When I went into the Army, etc.

QUEEN: They got me in the cookhouse,
Peeling taters I would be.
Spud - BASH! Spud - BASH!

KING: Spit - polish, etc.,

JIMOTHY: Left, right, etc.

ALL: Hurrah for the Milit'ry!

PHIDDLE & PHADDLE: When I went into the Army, etc.

PHIDDLE They put me into transport
And a driver I would be.
Grrr - CRASH! Grrr - CRASH!

QUEEN: Spud - BASH! Etc.,

KING: Spit - polish, etc.,

JIMOTHY: Left, right, etc.

ALL: Hurrah for the Milit'ry!

PHADDLE: When I went into the Army, etc.
They put me on Artillery
And firing I would be
Whee - BANG! Whee - BANG!

PHIDDLE: Grrr - CRASH! Etc.,

QUEEN: Spud - BASH! Etc.,

KING: Spit - polish, etc.,

JIMOTHY:	Left, right, etc.
ALL:	Hurrah for the Milit'ry!

(Enter MARY backwards L., as a drum-majorette, twirling stick, followed by NEDDY backwards wearing a bearskin helmet. Others move down below tab line.)

MARY:	When I went into the Army, etc. They put me into Cavalry And riding I would be - Whoa, Neddy! Whoa, Neddy!

(Close traverse tabs. Fly in frontcloth for Scene Nine, if used.)

PHADDLE:	Whee - BANG! Etc.,
PHIDDLE:	Grrr - CRASH! Etc.,
QUEEN:	Spud - BASH! Etc.,
KING:	Spit - polish, Etc.,
JIMOTHY:	Left, right, etc.
ALL:	Hurrah for the Milit'ry!

(Final march off, with MARY leading backwards and QUEEN bringing up the rear on NEDDY.

BLACKOUT.

Open traverse tabs.

MUSIC 47.)

II - 9 - 75

Scene Nine - ON THE WAY TO GRISLYKEEP

(Tabs or frontcloth, a woodland path (could use Scene Two cloth). Signpost painted in middle pointing L., reading "TO GRISLYKEEP" or signpost put on in blackout. Dim light to start. MUSIC 47 continues under opening dialogue. Enter PHILIP R.)

PHILIP: Come on, Puss, nearly there now, but hurry, Puss, hurry! (exit L.)

PUSS: (off R.) Master! Master!

(Enter R., carrying a bundle. Fade music.)

Dear, dear, I hope I haven't lost him. He will rush into things without thinking and that's no way to deal with an Ogre. I, however, have used my brain and the result is - this bundle. It doesn't look much, I know, but it's a do-it-yourself Ogre-killing-outfit. You'll see what I mean when I get to the castle, but I must hurry on in case Master does anything rash. Master! Master! (exit L.)

(Enter KING R.)

KING: Left - er, and right - er - (sees signpost) Mark - er (marks time) Yes, this is the - er. For - er (marches forward) Left - er and the other - er. (exit L.)

(PHADDLE enters R.)

PHADDLE: Left, right. Left, right.

(PHIDDLE enters R., pulling on a rope.

PHIDDLE: You can stop that now. We've deserted. Come on, Neddy. We must get to the castle before the others.

PHADDLE: Why?

PHIDDLE: To collect our reward for kidnapping the Princess, of course. The Ogre won't give us one if she's been rescued, will he? Come on, Neddy.

(Exit L., still pulling on rope, so that it is now stretched across stage.)

PHADDLE: I'm sorry we've deserted. I liked being a soldier. I wonder if I could train my guppies to march? (looks at rope then off R.) I don't think Neddy can have left home yet. (moving L.) Hey, Phiddle! Wait for me! Phiddle!

(PHIDDLE enters R. on the other end of the rope.)

PHIDDLE: Yes? Hm, that's funny, I've been this way before. Where's Neddy then?

(NEDDY enters L., with one end of the rope round his neck.)

NEDDY: Ee-aw!

PHADDLE: He must have taken a short cut.

PHIDDLE: Yes, well, lead on, Neddy.

(NEDDY backs off L.)

PHADDLE: I think he's got a touch of the Mistress Mary's.

(They exit L.)

JIMOTHY: (off R.) Left, right. Left, right.

(MISTRESS MARY enters backwards R., face to face with JIMOTHY.)

MARY: No, no. Right, left. Right, left.

JIMOTHY: All right. Right, left. Right left.

MARY: No, that seems wrong, too.

(They stop C.)

JIMOTHY: Ah, I know. (starting to march again) That side, this side. That side, this side.

(They almost collide with KING who enters L.)

KING: Oops! Oh, there you all - er - well, some of - er - Where's Queenie and the two - er - with the donkey?

JIMOTHY: We don't know, we've lost them, too.

KING: Then we must - er, mustn't we? Follow - er I mean, quick - er - let's go.

(They exit L. QUEEN enters in auditorium.)

QUEEN: Left, right, left, right. Halt! (halts) I'm afraid we're lost. (looks behind her) Oh no, I'm lost by myself. And no wonder, when it's so dark.

(HOUSE LIGHTS UP. Fade up stage lighting to fall.)

Ah, the sun's risen. (moving toward front) Well, I never, I'm with all those charming sitting-down people. I'm so glad you're still here. You must be anticipating a long stay, I see you've brought your food with you. Chocolates, such a sensible diet, especially for a figure like mine. Oh, might I have one? How very kind of you. Um, delicious! I'm sorry to have to eat and run, but I'd better get up there and see if I can find the others.

(Moves over cat-walk onto stage. HOUSE LIGHTS OUT.)

Dear me, what a very short day you have. (looks off L., then off R.) No, no sign of the others. I'll wait a bit and see if they turn up. Now, what can I do while I'm waiting? I know, I'll sing a song. What song do you think I ought to sing, (CONDUCTOR's name)?

(A piece of sheet music drops behind her from flies as she speaks to CONDUCTOR.)

CONDUCTOR: How about that one behind you?

QUEEN: What? (turns) Oh, how very opportune. Could I have a little of your excellent music?

CONDUCTOR: Certainly.

MUSIC 48. "ORANGE YOLK"

QUEEN: Jaffa hear the story of one old Mother Hen?
She went and laid an orange, then laid another ten.
Each time she laid an orange the little chicks hoorayed,
And one chick said to the other little chicks,
"Look what Marmalade!"

Very nice. And now I'll give you the surprise of your lives. I'm going to ask you to sing it with me. It's a pity we haven't got a larger copy -

(The song sheet drops from flies, in front of sheet music. Fly out sheet music.)

What a bit of luck, we have. It's written in quite easy Marmaladian so I'm sure you'll be able to manage it. Let's try, anyway. All together now. (lets them sing a few bars) Ah no. I don't think you quite understood. I said all together. That's Marmaladian for everybody. Away we go then.

(They sing it through.)

Not bad. Not at all bad. But I'm sure you can do better still. If only the others were here to help you. Silly me. I know how I can find them, it'll help to get your voices working too. I'll go and take a silver bell.

(Moves to do so. EFFECT 26. BELLS JINGLE. AUDIENCE shout. HOUSE LIGHTS UP as JIMOTHY, MARY and KING enter in auditorium.)

ALL 3: Left, right. Left, right.

QUEEN: I knew that would do the trick. And how nice, the sun's risen again. I'm just getting all these clever people to do a little singing, dears. Do you think you could help them?

JIMOTHY: Yes, but why don't you get the children up there to help you, your Majesty?

QUEEN: The children? Up here? Oh, do you think they would?

JIMOTHY: I'm jolly sure of it.

(He and the others encourage children onto stage and help them up. Ad lib with children singing and helping them down again.)

QUEEN: All back? Good. Well, you'd better come up here now dears and we'll all of us, every single one of us, sing it just once more. All ready?

(Close traverse tabs, fly out cloth and song sheet as it is sung through for last time. They exit L., waving as they go.

BLACKOUT.

Open traverse tabs.)

Scene Ten - GRISLYKEEP, THE OGRE'S CASTLE

(Fullset suggestive of a Magician's den. Cut-out ground-row of shelves laden with bottles set at back of rostrum. Wing L. painted as a huge refrigerator and inscribed with a suitable trade name or "REFRIGERATOR" on a practical door in it. Wing R. representing a hooded fireplace with a cauldron hanging over fire. R.C. chair and table, with phials, bottles, a huge book entitled "MAGIC", a magic wand and a high wizard's hat on it. Mysterious **MUSIC 49**. The OGRE GREEDYGUTS discovered asleep in chair at table. He should look very tall and can add to his height with a built-up bald wig and built-up boots. He also wears whiskers and a wizard's robe. PHILIP creeps on L.)

PHILIP: The Ogre!

(OGRE stirs in his sleep. PHILIP draws sword. OGRE subsides again.)

No sign of Esmerelda. She's probably locked away somewhere. I'll take a look round.

(Creeps up to rostrum. OGRE stirs again, PHILIP makes ready to defend himself, but OGRE subsides once more and PHILIP creeps off R. on rostrum. OGRE stretches and yawns.

OGRE: Hm, must have dozed off. (takes a large hour glass on a chain from inner pocket.) Time for din-dins. (claps hands) Vassals!

(5 CHORUS enter as OGRE's VASSALS.)

VASSALS: Yes, O master?

OGRE: Food.

VASSALS: There isn't any, O master.

1st V: Nothing in the larder.

2nd V: Nothing in the Fridge.

3rd V: And months to wait before you can steal the next Orange harvest.

OGRE: Silence, you vile vassal! I never steal. It's just that people will leave oranges hanging on trees and they happen to drop into my hand. But I want food now. Isn't there anything?

4th V: Well, there's that Princess the Demon brought the other day, O master.

OGRE: You know I don't like eating people. I only eat fruit. Vanish Vassals and leave me to my magic. I'll try to create a food.

VASSALS: Yes, O master. (They exit R.)

OGRE: (puts on wizards hat and flips through pages of book) Now let me see. Hm. (flips over more pages) Doesn't look too promising. Oh, if only I didn't have to be so careful about my diet, I might enjoy being an Ogre.

MUSIC 50. "BEING AN OGRE"

OGRE:
> If food weren't the constant question
> And I ate all that I could see
> Without getting indigestion,
> I'd enjoy being old me.
> If I could just take it easy,
> On a tank-full of cream for tea,
> Without feeling kind of queasy
> I'd enjoy being old me.
>
> I burp on au gratin cauliflowers;
> I'm sick on a sixpenny bit of skate;
> And one thing that depresses me for hours,
> Is a pound and a half of fat upon my plate.
>
> Compared with all other giants
> I've the appetite of a flea;
> But it's no use to show defiance -
> It's no joke
> Being a bloke
> Such as an Ogre like me.

(closes book) No luck. Looks as though it may have to be the Princess, after all. I gave her a special potion to fatten her up, just in case - I told her it was for slimming. Wonder how it's working? (calling to R.) Princess! Come here!

PRINCESS: (off R.) I'm coming, Ogre, and I'm very cross.

(PRINCESS enters R., wearing an ox's head.

Just look what your wretched potion has done. Slimming indeed! Do something about it, Ogre.

OGRE: Don't you talk to me like that, or I'll leave you just as you are.

PRINCESS: You mean you're not clever enough to change me back.

OGRE: What! I certainly am. (takes a phial and pours various ingredients into it, muttering to himself) Impudent baggage! Good mind to turn her into a pomegranate and gobble her up right away. Not clever enough indeed! There. Drink that, restore you to normal immediately.

PRINCESS: It had jolly well better. (drinks)

(BLACKOUT. WHITE FLASH. Screech from PRINCESS. She exits R. Lights up.)

OGRE: You see - good gracious! I've made her disappear! (hastily flips through book)

(Enter PRINCESS R. now with an ass's head.)

PRINCESS: And I suppose you think this is an improvement? I said you weren't clever enough.

OGRE: How dare you! I'll show you! (hurriedly mixing more

OGRE: (continued - ingredients in a phial) I'll -

(EFFECTS 27. Door knock off L.)

Callers? Strange. See who it is, while I'm mixing this.

PRINCESS: (crossing L.) Very well, but I'm not one of your Vassals, you know. I'm your very unwilling prisoner. And no mistakes this time. (exit L.)

OGRE: Impertinent hussy!

NEDDY: (off L.) Ee-aw!

(PRINCESS runs on L., chased by NEDDY, braying happily, followed by PHIDDLE and PHADDLE chasing NEDDY. PRINCESS runs anti-clockwise round stage.)

PRINCESS: Help! Ogre, do something!)
Quickly! Help!
) (together)
PHIDDLE &
PHADDLE: Come back! Neddy, come here, etc.)

OGRE: I'm being as quick as I can! (nevertheless speeds up mixing operations) This, that, that, this, squeeze of lemon, salt, pepper, vinegar - (thrusts phial into PRINCESS's hand as she passes) Here, take this!

PRINCESS: About time! (runs off R.)

OGRE: (picks up wand and waves it) Stop!

(NEDDY, PHIDDLE and PHADDLE stop abruptly.)

What's the meaning of this? Who are you?

PHIDDLE: We're Phiddle and Phaddle and we've called to collect our reward. You know, the one that that very ancient gent said you'd give us for kidnapping the Princess.

OGRE: You mean that doddering old fool Demon Oldbad? Fellow's senile. Knows perfectly well I wouldn't give a reward for anything.

PHIDDLE: What!

PHADDLE: There, I knew it. Let's get out of here.

(NEDDY nods and he and PHADDLE start to go. OGRE puts up wand.)

OGRE: Wait! Just had an idea. Now you're here I will reward you.

PHIDDLE: See?

OGRE: Yes, with the special honour of becoming - (pointing at them) - tomorrow's breakfast - (pointing at NEDDY) - and tomorrow's dinner.

PHIDDLE &
PHADDLE: What!)
(together)
NEDDY: Ee-aw!)

II - 10 - 81

OGRE: Yes, you'll make a couple of very nice grapefruit and he'll be a splendid melon. You'd better go in the fridge to keep fresh.

(Waves wand at them. MUSIC 51. They turn like automatons and move towards fridge. OGRE points wand at door and it opens for them. When they have disappeared inside he points wand again and door shuts. (door operated by thin nylon lines pulled from offstage.))

Excellent, now I shan't have to eat the Princess. Not yet anyway. Wonder if she's transformed back again? (moves D.R., stops by plant) Hm, never noticed that before. Think I'll take one.

(Puts out hand. EFFECTS 28. BELLS JINGLE. AUDIENCE shout. JIMOTHY puts head on L.)

JIMOTHY: Are you mad? (withdraws head)

OGRE: Don't know what you're all shouting about, but I'll turn the lot of you into cox's orange pippins if you're not careful.

(Stomps off R. QUEEN looks on L.)

QUEEN: (whispering) Ah, all clear now. (withdraws head) Come on, Army.

(QUEEN, KING, JIMOTHY, and MARY - backwards - creep-march on L. The following scene is done in whispers until the OGRE's re-entry.)

ALL: Left right, left right, etc.

QUEEN: Army, halt!

(They halt. VASSALS 1- 4 creep-march on L. above them, VASSAL 4 backwards. They carry short spears and looped ropes.)

VASSALS: Left right, left right, etc.

1st V: Army, halt.

(VASSALS halt, directly behind others, who look at each other puzzled and uneasy.)

QUEEN: Army, left turn!

(They turn L., MARY R.)

1st V: Army, left turn!

(VASSALS turn L., 4th VASSAL R.)

QUEEN: Seems to be something of an echo here.

KING: Er - yes.

2nd V: Er - no.

(OTHERS look at each other as before. JIMOTHY starts to tremble and his knees knock together, assisted by DRUMMER on wood block.

JIMOTHY: I th-th-think there's somebody else here.

QUEEN: Nonsense.

1st V:	Absolute nonsense.
JIMOTHY:	What's that ker - ker - ker - nocking then?
3rd V:	Your ker - ker - ker - nees.

(5th VASSAL enters L., with spear.)

5th V:	(in ordinary voice) What are you doing?
OTHER V:	Ssh!
OTHERS:	Yes, ssh! Eh? (they turn and look over their shoulders) Aah!
VASSALS:	Hullo!

(VASSALS drop their looped ropes over the OTHERS. KING drops halberd. OGRE enters L., with PRINCESS now herself again.)

OGRE:	You see, I told you it would -
PRINCESS:	Father! Mother!)
KING & QUEEN:	Esmerelda!) (together)
JIM & MARY:	The Ogre!)
OGRE:	What's going on here? Thought you Vassals said there wasn't any food in the house?
1st V:	An unexpected delivery, O Master.
OGRE:	Put them in the fridge then. Oh no, it's full. Into the larder with 'em.
PRINCESS:	Ogre! Release them instantly!) (together)
OTHERS:	Hey, wait, you can't put us -)
OGRE:	Silence! Vassals, vamoose!
VASSALS:	Yes, O Master.

(They prod the others off L.)

QUEEN:	Ow! What vicious vassals!
OGRE:	Beastly strangers charging in without so much as a by-your-leave. Still, that's dealt with all of them.

(PHILIP enters U.R. on rostrum, sword drawn.)

PHILIP:	Not quite!
PRINCESS:	Philip!
OGRE:	Another of 'em! I'll soon settle you, you young puppy! (picks up KING's halberd) Take that!

(MUSIC 52. Lunges at PHILIP, misses him. PHILIP pricks him with sword as he jumps aside.)

Ow! That hurt!

II - 10 - 83

(Lunges again and misses, fight develops with PHILIP gaining the advantage till he disarms OGRE and forces him back over table.)

PHILIP: Ogre, will you surrender or shall I run you through?

OGRE: (picking up wand) Neither! Drop that sword!

(Waves wand. Sword drops from PHILIP's hand.)

Vassals!

(1st and 2nd VASSALS enter R.)

Seize them!

VASSALS: (doing so) Yes, O master.

OGRE: I'll put you two safely under lock and key myself. Come on, you vapid vassals, away with them.

(VASSALS hustle a struggling PHILIP and PRINCESS off R. PUSS looks on L. and watches them off.)

(following) Obstreperous pair. That young pipsqueak nearly did for me. (exit)

PUSS: (entering) Evidently I've arrived just in time. (takes from his bundle a short wizard's cloak and a little wizard's hat which he proceeds to put on) This is my Ogre killing outfit I was telling you about. It doesn't do anything in itself, but it's so important to be properly dressed for each occasion, I feel.

(OGRE enters R.)

OGRE: Another intruder! (raises wand threateningly) Why I -

PUSS: (bowing low) The mighty Wizard Greedyguts, I presume.

OGRE: (lowering wand) Er - what?

PUSS: (moving forward and shaking his hand warmly) This is a great honour. I have long looked forward to meeting you, Wizard Greedyguts. Your fame has spread far and wide among we wizards.

OGRE: Really? Uncommon civil of you. I didn't know there were any cat wizards, though.

PUSS: Ah, silly of me, I should have explained. I have merely assumed the form of a cat. Transformation is an aspect of wizardry I'm particularly interested in. Do you do much yourself in that line?

OGRE: Oh, yes indeed. Mostly people into fruit.

PUSS: Ah, interesting, but what about people into animals?

OGRE: Hah! Easy stuff!

PUSS: But self transformation. I'm sure you can't do that so easily.

OGRE: What! Course I can. (busily mixes some ingredients in a phial at R. of table) Simple as A. B. - er - H. Watch this. (dips wand

OGRE: (continued - into phial and touches himself with it.)

(Music ting. FLASH. BLACKOUT. OGRE exits. A LION takes his place. (This could be played by one of the CHORUS.) LIGHTS UP. LION roars and advances menacingly towards PUSS who hurriedly jumps onto chair.)

PUSS: Aah! Yes - er - very good.

(Shrinks back as LION roars and waves a paw at him.)

E-excellent. But it's a little difficult to talk when you're roaring so much.

(FLASH. BLACKOUT. LION exits. OGRE re-enters. LIGHTS UP.)

OGRE: (laughing heartily) That scared you, eh? Made you jump a bit.

PUSS: Not at all. I merely jumped up here to see whether the transformation was quite complete. And I must admit it wasn't bad, not bad at all.

OGRE: Not bad! Not bad!

PUSS: Well, I mean, you're such a big man, it's simple for you to turn yourself into a big animal. But could you turn yourself into something very small - say a mouse, for instance? Now that would be really clever.

OGRE: A mouse? Easy as winking, don't even need to mix anything.

(Touches himself with wand. Music ting. SMALL FLASH. BLACKOUT. Exit OGRE. LIGHTS UP. Small clockwork mouse enters squeaking L.)

PUSS: Yes, that is clever, Ogre. But perhaps not as clever as you thought! (leaps on mouse and kills it) I've killed him!

(EFFECTS 29. THUNDER ROLL. LIGHTS FLICKER. VASSALS run shrieking from R. to L. PUSS holds up mouse in triumph.)

The wicked Ogre Greedyguts is dead!

(Removes wizard outfit as PHILIP and PRINCESS run on R. and KING, QUEEN, JIMOTHY and MARY L.)

ALL: What's happened? We're free! We're free! Puss!

PUSS: (bowing) At your service. Welcome to the castle of my master the Marquess of Carabas.

OTHERS: What?

PHILIP: No, Puss, let's tell the truth. This isn't my castle and I'm not a Marquess. I'm just Philip the Miller's son. But, Princess - Esmerelda, I love you as much as any Marquess could. Will you marry me?

PRINCESS: No.

(MUSIC 53. SPRITE pants on R.)

SPRITE: I knew it, late again, oh blow!
I simply can't have you say "no".

SPRITE:	(continued) But once the Demon's spell is broke, Mayhap your answer you'll revoke And thus my hopes for him fulfil. Now will you wed him?

(Touches PRINCESS with wand. Music ting.)

PRINCESS:	Yes, I will! For commoners I much prefer.
PUSS:	I trust your love 'twill not deter To learn then that he's noble born. He was of lands and title shorn When this same Ogre I have here - (twiddles mouse in hand) His father to his death did steer And stole his castle and estate.
SPRITE:	(to PHILIP) Puss saved you from a sim'lar fate. You were a babe so kitten-like, He carried you o'er field and dyke Until the Miller's door was reach'd.
PUSS:	That kind man's heart was easy breach'd, And when at last he went to rest He left to you an oaken chest Which held some things I'd chanc'd to gain When once this rogue had sleeping lain, Those things which prove my story true, Your erstwhile brothers stole from you.
SPRITE:	Don't worry, Puss, I got them back. (producing them) One robe, a little fray'd alack, One coronet and jewels galore.
QUEEN:	Well! What a splendid son-in-law.
PHILIP:	So that's why those two turn'd on me. But where I wonder can they be?

(Moans from PHIDDLE and PHADDLE in fridge.)

JIMOTHY:	Oo-er!
MARY:	There's something there inside.
JIMOTHY:	But what?
SPRITE:	The answer I'll provide.

(Waves her wand at fridge. MUSIC 54. Door slowly opens and PHIDDLE and PHADDLE emerge with frozen gait, frosted with snow, and bearded with icicles. Icicles also dangle from their hands and ears etc.)

QUEEN:	Help! Snowmen most abominable!
KING:	Yes, let's take ref - er - 'neath the table!

(He and QUEEN dive under table. NEDDY emerges from fridge also icicled and frosted. Door shuts behind him.)

JIMOTHY: Ow! Here's a donkey yeti too!

PHIDDLE: No, we're not snowmen.

PHADDLE: We're - achoo!

(KING and QUEEN emerge.)

SPRITE: 'Tis Philip's one time brethren twain!
Whose guilt, alas, is very plain.

PHIDDLE: Well, mine is, but young Phaddle here
I drove to it by threats, I fear.
But I shall now a new leaf turn
And will henceforth my living earn.

PHILIP: Then I'll forgiveness not withold,
For all you've gain'd's a nasty cold.

PHADDLE: Well, let's get home now that's arranged,
My guppies need their water chang'd.

PHIDDLE: Right. Neddy, come!

NEDDY: Ee-aw! Achoo!

PHIDDLE: Hullo, he's caught a corker too.

(Exit PHIDDLE, PHADDLE and NEDDY L.)

QUEEN: Now Marmaduke, I think 'twere wise
We should the wedding plans devise.

KING: Planning? That's what old Snoozle's for.

QUEEN: But Snoozle's lost.

(Snore from SNOOZLE in fridge.)

Was that a snore?

(SPRITE points wand at door. MUSIC 55. SNOOZLE emerges yawning with a picnic basket, also covered with snow and icicles.)

JIMOTHY: Fresh frozen Snoozle, I declare!

SNOOZLE: Well, bless my woolly underwear,
It's cold. Ah, sorry, slight delay,
I think I must have lost my way.
Still here's the picnic food and booze. (yawns)
Excuse me while I have a snooze.

(Puts basket down and exits L. yawning.)

QUEEN: I think in view of all these naps
Lord of the Bedchamber, perhaps,
A better post for him would be.
Which leaves the Chamb'lain's office free.

		II - 10 - 87

KING:	Then let us Jim - er - well, promote.
JIMOTHY:	Oh, yippee, yes!
KING:	Your thanks we note.
JIMOTHY:	(kneeling at MARY's feet) And now I feel that I can ask -
MARY:	(pulling him up) No, no, that is the woman's task. (kneels at his feet) Oh, Jimothy, please say you will.
JIMOTHY:	This is so sudden - heart be still! I cannot cause a maid distress And so, of course, the answer's "yes".

(He pulls her to her feet to kiss her, but she bends him back in a passionate embrace.)

SPRITE:	Now all is well, and that 'tis so Our thanks to Puss must chiefly go
PUSS:	My modesty but lets me say, That you're quite right.
PHILIP: ALL:	Here, here, hooray!

MUSIC 56. MEDLEY

PUSS:	With intellect empirical, Loquacity so lyrical It's not at all a miracle, Not by the longest chalk. Your ideas were all out of date. I hope you now appreciate That CATS CAN TALK!
CHORUS:	Since your words you haven't minced We now are utterly convinced That CATS CAN TALK!
QUEEN & KING:	For the Ogre we'd like to state We wouldn't give two hoots. We intend to celebrate - All thanks to Puss in Boots.
CHORUS:	It's holiday in Marmaladia. Let its happiness never fade here. Let us all go madly gay, dear, Let's go out and play Upon this lovely holiday.

(BLACKOUT.

Close traverse tabs.)

Scene Eleven – REWARDS AND FAIRIES

(Tabs. BLUE SPOT UP L. MUSIC 57. Enter a very dejected DEMON. BLUE FLASH L. immediately. He regards it with disfavour.)

DEMON: It would! Now 'tis too late, alack,
Yes, yes, they've given me the sack.
Too old, they had the nerve to say!
And just to prove that crime don't pay,
They've gone and cut my pension down –
To half a counterfeited crown.

(MUSIC 58. Enter SPRITE R., with wings and full-sized wand.)

SPRITE: Oh, Demon, look! I've won them! Wheee! (twirls round to show him.)

DEMON: The wing'd victory, I see.

SPRITE: Now all I need's to learn to fly.

DEMON: And I another job to try.

SPRITE: Then why not come and work for good?

DEMON: Oh, no! And yet... D'you think I could?

SPRITE: Yes. I gain'd Fairy rank last night,
So there's a vacancy for Sprite.
D'you fancy that?

DEMON: What would I do?

SPRITE: Run errands, make the honeydew.
But later, when you're used to things,
You too could try to win your wings.

DEMON: All right. I will!

SPRITE: Give me your hand,
And welcome to our Fairy band.

(They shake hands.)

Now I've a task for you straightway.
(puts out hands for a parcel to be put into it from R. Imperiously.) Deliver this, without delay!

DEMON: (touching forelock)
Yes, very good, ma'am. Who's it for?
(looks at label)
Sprite Oldbad. You mean – me?

(SPRITE relaxes, grins broadly and nods.)

Oh, cor! (starts to sniffle)
I'm sorry, but this is, you see,
The only present given me
In all my long nine thousand years.

II - 11 - 89

SPRITE:	Poor Demon – Sprite! But dry your tears, And ope' the parcel.
DEMON:	Yes, I will. I say, this really is a thrill! (takes halo out of parcel.) Oh.
SPRITE:	Do you like it? Come, confess.
DEMON:	Just what I've always wanted. Yes.
SPRITE:	But does it fit?

(DEMON puts it on.)

Is it too tight?
It's six and seven eighths.

DEMON: Just right.
And now I am allow'd this side,
There's just one thing I've never tried.

(Moves to bell plant. EFFECT 30. BELLS JINGLE. AUDIENCE shout. JIMOTHY runs on R., DEMON hastily retreats L., leaving SPRITE by plant.)

JIMOTHY: What, something at my plant once more?
Well, thank you very much, I'm sure.
I s'pose it was this butterfly. (points to FAIRY)

DEMON: Yes! (remembers halo)
No. I cannot tell a lie.
I tried to steal a bell or two.

JIMOTHY: You naughty old delinquent you.
Well, more temptation I'll remove.
(Detaches head of plant. Moves L.)
Besides it will most useful prove.
I have to find my bride a ring,
So this should be the very thing. (exit L.)

DEMON: Oh dear, now what am I to say?
Forgive me, Fairy dear, I pray.
Nine thousand years of doing wrong
Has form'd a habit rather strong.

SPRITE: I know, but I don't think you should
Try all at once to be too good.

MUSIC 59. "WHAT'S THE GOOD?"

BOTH: What's the good of happiness unless you can be sad?
What's the good of being sane if not a little mad?
And what's the good of goodness if there isn't any bad?
What good am I without you?
What's the good of waking if you haven't been asleep?

BOTH:	(continued) What's the use of laughter if you've never learned to weep? There would be no shallow end unless there were a deep - What good am I without you?
SPRITE:	You're not quite as black as paint.
DEMON:	You, I'm sure, are not a saint Things seem often what they ain't!
SPRITE:	Really on the level, I'm a little devil.
BOTH:	What's the good of blackness if you've never known the white? What's the good of morning if there hasn't been a night? And what's the good of Demons if there weren't a little Sprite? What's the good, What's the good, What good am I without you?

(Exeunt L. and R. MUSIC 60. Traverse tabs OPEN for Scene Twelve.)

II - 12 - 91

Scene Twelve - THE WEDDING RECEPTION OF THE MARQUESS AND MARCHIONESS OF CARABAS

(Fullstage. Grand palace setting. Steps down in C. of rostrum. Wings L. and R. CHORUS enter from L. and R. on rostrum in pairs. Each pair meets in C. of rostrum and comes D.C. to take their bow. They then split and back away to form diagonal lines L. and R. The principals follow a similar procedure forming diagonal lines in front of CHORUS. SPRITE from R. and backing R., and DEMON from L., backing L., ROWLEY from R., backing R., OGRE from L., backing L., SNOOZLE from R., backing R., NEDDY from L., backing L., PHIDDLE from R., backing R., and PHADDLE from L., backing R., MARY from R., backing R., KING from L., backing L., JIMOTHY from R., backing R., QUEEN from L.. backing L., PUSS from R., backing L. MUSIC 61. Fanfare. All turn in as PHILIP enters from L. and PRINCESS from R. and meet in C. of rostrum.)

ALL: Hurray!

(PHILIP and PRINCESS move D.C. to take their bow. PRINCIPALS move down into a straight line with them. CHORUS move up onto rostrum.)

PHILIP:
    The time has come to part, good friends,
    For this is where our story ends.
    Fortunes -

MARY & PRINCESS: Brides -

SPRITE: And wings -

PHILIP: Are won.

DEMON: And I've at last with evil done.

PUSS:
    These human folk talk such a lot,
    While I, a cat, of course, do not.
    It's just "goodbye" they want to say.

QUEEN: But in a Marmaladian way!

MUSIC 62. "MARMALADIA"

ALL:
    And so farewell to Marmaladia,
    What a shame you could not have stayed here:
    We wish every gent and lady a
        Future that is bright.
    We all hope, as you homeward are wending
    All your tales have as happy an ending.
    We, the folks of Marmaladia,
        Played for your delight.
    Now we bid you all GOODNIGHT.

(CURTAIN.)

FURNITURE AND PROPERTY PLOT
PART ONE

Set on stage throughout: Large flower pot in front of Proscenium arch R. Inside it plant with little silver bells, which is made to "grow" by pulling on a thin nylon line attached to the head of the plant and then threaded offstage.

Scene One

Set on stage: Large flour sack C.

Off L.

Large prop silver bell with small practical bell and detachable prop clapper fitted inside. 3 scrolls.	JIMOTHY
Soap box go-cart with hooter attached. (This should be just like go-carts made by children from old boxes and pram wheels)	KING & QUEEN
*Prop lampost	To fall on.
Small practical flash box and matches	DEMON
Old woollen shawl	To be thrown on to DEMON
Replica of will	DEMON
Lantern of lampost to go over head	KING

Off R.

Rope	PHIDDLE & PHADDLE
Dog-eared copy of will	PHIDDLE
*Prop lampost	To fall on

*These lamposts can be pin-hinged to the stage behind the wings and pushed to fall over, then whisked upright and out of sight again by thin nylon lines attached to them.

Off Behind Mill L.C.

Saddle and bridle	PHADDLE
Brass and oak chest with: Golden Guinea, red robe trimmed with ermine, coronet and bag containing jewels	PHIDDLE & PHADDLE
Bucket of water and saucer of milk	PHADDLE
Top hat with large crepe mourning band and bow	PHIDDLE

PERSONAL

SPRITE	Very short wand

Scene Two

Set on stage: Clump of dandelions with detachable leaves L.

Off R.

False nose, moustache and glasses, cap, cobbler's leather apron, stool, hammer, old shoe and bag containing red boots.	SPRITE

Off L.

Check PUSS has the guinea.

BEHIND BACK CLOTH

3 prop rabbits to be pushed through on cue.

Scene Three

Set on Stage: Double throne on small dais U.L.C. covered with dust sheet.
Sceptre and orb set on throne.
Gilt and plush chair to L., of throne.

Off L.

List and pencil	QUEEN
2 buckets, 2 brooms, some dusters and a prop floor polisher fitted with castors	JIMOTHY
Large prop cylinder type vacuum cleaner fitted with wheels and hose to squirt water (Rubber tubing goes from the nozzle through the hose and the cylinder, at the end of which it appears as the lead and goes offstage to a pump).	KING
Feather duster	KING
Handkerchief	JIMOTHY
Vase with flowers upside down	MARY
Miniature combinations	ROWLEY

Off R.

Grip with prop iron inside it.	ROWLEY
Mop and bucket of water	MARY
Wand of office	SNOOZLE
Huge visiting card	PHIDDLE

Check PUSS has shoe bag containing rabbits

PERSONAL

KING	Knotted handkerchief under crown.

Scene Four

Off L.

Bag of jewels	PHIDDLE
Coronet and robe	PHADDLE
Long cloak and hat with Pawnbroker 3 ball sign	
Tray with trinkets, jeweller's eyepeice and notice: "D. OLDBAD ITINERANT PAWNBROKER"	
Bag of money and beard	DEMON

Off R.

Long cloak and hat with Pawnbroker 3 ball sign	
Tray with trinkets and notice: "S. YOUNGOOD ITINERANT PAWNBROKER"	
Bag of money and beard	SPRITE

Scene Five

Set on stage: Large dandelion with seed head growing R., on rostrum.

Off L.

Large beach ball	JIMOTHY
KING & QUEEN's costumes	CHORUS
Large skip for picnic basket	ROWLEY
Bundle of clothes	ROWLEY
Binoculars on a strap, pistol and a cosh	PHIDDLE
Pistol, a cosh and 2 black masks without eyeholes	PHADDLE

PART TWO

Scene Six

Set on stage: Double throne in C., of rostrum

Off R.

2 music stands and sheet music	PHIDDLE & PHADDLE
1 large instrument case with conductor's baton inside it	PHIDDLE
1 large instrument case with small triangle inside it	PHADDLE
Small gilt chair	PHADDLE
Notebook and pencil	PHIDDLE

Chloroform bottle and pad	PHIDDLE

Scene Seven

Off R.

Pair of PUSS's red boots (to fit PHADDLE)	PHADDLE

Scene Eight

Set on stage: D.L. a rack containing a rifle, a halberd, a sword, in a scabbard with a belt, 2 bearskin helmets hanging above rack. D.L. a prop cannon with a slender detachable barrel with a pile of rubber and cotton wool balls beside it. (Barrel can be made from chicken wire with 3 or 4 thicknesses of thin cardboard round it and covered by painted canvas.), blunderbuss and large bunch of keys for JIMOTHY, bugle on R. wing.

Off R.

Small piece of material	MARY

Scene Nine

Off R.

A bundle containing short wizard's cloak and a little wizard's hat	PUSS
Long rope	PHIDDLE

Scene Ten

Set on stage: R.C. chair and a table with phials, bottles, a huge book entitled "MAGIC", magic wand and high wizard's hat.

PERSONAL

OGRE	Large hourglass on a chain.

Off R.

Ox's head	PRINCESS
Ass's head	PRINCESS

Off L.

5 spears and 4 looped ropes	CHORUS (as vassals)
Small clockwork mouse to be sent on stage	
Prop icicles (these can be made from cellophane) and snow (sliver glitter)	PHIDDLE & PHADDLE NEDDY & SNOOZLE
Picnic basket	SNOOZLE

Scene Eleven

Off R.

Full sized wand	SPRITE

Parcel handed onto SPRITE and containing halo for the DEMON fitted onto a headband by an upright supporting piece.

EFFECTS PLOT
PART ONE
Scene One

1.	Bells jingle	Off R.
2.	" "	"
3.	" "	"
4.	" "	"
5.	" "	"
6.	" "	"
7.	" "	"
8.	Banging and clattering	Off L.
9.	Clatter	"
10.	Loud glass crash (bucket of broken glass thrown into second bucket)	Off R.
11.	Loud glass crash	Off L.
12.	Bells jingle	Off R.
13.	Glass crash	Off L.
14.	" "	"
15.	Bells jingle	Off R.

Scene Three

16.	Clock chiming half-hour	Grams.
17.	Bells jingle	Off R.
18.	Thud of body falling	Off L.
19.	Clock striking three	Grams

Scene Five

20.	Alarm clock bell ringing	Off R.
21.	Bird singing (bird whistle)	"
22.	" "	Off L.
23.	Bells jingle	Off R.

N.B. If preferred tape can, of course, be used instead of grams.

PART TWO
Scene Six
24.	Bells jingle	Off R.
25.	Gong	"

Scene Nine
26.	Bells jingle	"

Scene Ten
27.	Door knock	Off L.
28.	Bells jingle	Off R.
29.	Thunder roll	As convenient

Scene Eleven
30.	Bells jingle	Off R.

MUSIC PLOT
PART ONE
1. Overture

Scene One
2.	Opening Chorus, "MARMALADIA"	Chorus
3.	Entrance music for Princess	Orch.
4.	"CHANGES"	Princess, Rowley and Chorus.
5.	Jimothy's entrance music	Orch.
6.	Mistress Mary's entrance music	"
7.	"THE WISE ONES"	Jimothy and Mary
8.	Phiddle and Phaddle entrance music	Orch.
9.	Neddy's entrance music	"
10.	Philip's entrance music	"
11.	Puss's entrance music	"
12.	"HOME"	Philip and Chorus
13.	King and Queen's entrance music	Orch.
14.	"ANTHEM"	King and Queen
15.	"WHOEVER YOU ARE"	Philip and Princess
16.	Sprite's music	Orch.
17.	Demon's music	"

18.	Higher education spell	Demon
19.	"MARMALADIA" reprise 2. (continue, orchestra only, as link to next scene).	Ensemble

Scene Two

20.	Sprite's music, reprise 16.	Orch.
21.	Music for tabs opening	"
22.	Rabbit popping music	"
23.	"WE'RE A TEAM!" (continue, orchestra only, as link to next scene).	Philip and Puss

Scene Three

24.	Processional march, "ANTHEM", reprise 14.	Orch.
25.	Princess's entrance, "ANTHEM", reprise 14.	"
26.	"TALKING CAT"	Puss and ensemble
27.	"TALKING CAT", reprise 26. (continue, orchestra only, as link to next scene and with Puss to open next scene).	" " "

Scene Four

28.	"TALKING CAT", reprise 26, for Puss and Philip's exit.	Orch.
29.	Sprite music, reprise 16	"
30.	"YAH! BOO! HISS!" (continue, orchestra only, as link to next scene)	Demon, Phiddle and Phaddle

Scene Five

31.	Ballet	Sprite and Chorus
32.	Neddy's music, reprise 9	Orch.
33.	Beach Ball Ballet	King, Queen and Jimothy
34.	"PALACE FOR TWO"	Philip and Princess
35.	Stealthy entrance music for Phiddle and Phaddle	Orch.
36.	"ANTHEM", reprise 14.	Esemble

PART TWO

37. Entr'acte.

Scene Six

38.	Fanfares and "TWISTED GAVOTTE"	Ensemble
39.	"WHOEVER YOU ARE", reprise 15	Philip and Princess
40.	"MISTRESS MARY QUITE CONTRARY"	Ensemble
41.	Sprite music, reprise 16	Orch.
42.	"FIND HER!" (continue, orchestra only as link to next scene)	Queen and Ensemble

Scene Seven

43.	Sprite music, reprise 16	Orch.
44.	Phiddle and Phaddle's music, reprise 8, for their exit and continue as link to next scene.	Orch.

Scene Eight

45.	"BLUNDERFUL LOVE"	Philip and Jimothy
46.	"HURRAH FOR THE MILITARY!"	King, Queen, Phiddle, Phaddle, Jimothy and Mary.
47.	"FIND HER", reprise 42, as link to next scene and as music under opening dialogue	Orch.

Scene Nine

48.	"ORANGE YOLK" (continue, orchestra only, as link to next scene)	Queen and Audience

Scene Ten

49.	Mysterious music	Orch.
50.	"BEING AN OGRE"	Ogre.
51.	Spell music	Orch.
52.	Fight music	"
53.	Sprite music, reprise 16	"
54.	Spell music, reprise 51	"
55.	" " " "	"
56.	Medley (continue, orchestra only, as link to next scene)	Ensemble

Scene Eleven

57.	Demon music, reprise 17, in slow tempo	Orch.
58.	Sprite music, reprise 16	"
59.	"WHAT'S THE GOOD?"	Sprite and Demon

60. "MARMALADIA", reprise 2 as link to
 next scene and continue as music for
 walk-down   Orch.

Scene Twelve

61. Fanfare   "

62. Grand Finale, "MARMALADIA",
 reprise 2   Tutti

www.ingramcontent.com/pod-product-compliance
Ingram Content Group UK Ltd.
Pitfield, Milton Keynes, MK11 3LW, UK
UKHW021843210426
5322IPUK00022B/445